How to Invest $50–$5,000

How to Invest $50-$5,000

Eighth Edition

The Small Investor's Step-by-Step
Plan for Low-Risk, High-Value Investing

Nancy Dunnan

Quill

A HarperResource Book

An Imprint of HarperCollins*Publishers*

While the method of investment described in this book is believed to be effective, there is no guarantee that the method will be profitable in specific applications, owing to the risk that is involved in investing of almost any kind. Thus, neither the publisher nor the author assume liability for any losses that may be sustained by the use of the method described in this book, and any such liability is hereby expressly disclaimed.

Designed by Lisa Diercks

Library of Congress Cataloging-in-Publication Data

Dunnan, Nancy.
    How to invest $50–$5,000 / Nancy Dunnan.—8th ed.
        p. cm.—(A HarperResource book)
    Includes index.
    ISBN 0-06-008779-X
        1. Investments—Handbooks, manuals, etc.   I. Title: How to invest fifty dollars–five thousand dollars.   II. Title.   III. Series.

HG4527 .D77 2003
332.67'8—dc21

2002068089

03 04 05 06 07 WB/RRD 10 9 8 7 6 5 4 3 2 1

Contents

Introduction: Getting the Most for Your Money   vii

Your Personal Financial Calendar   xii

Part One: Safe Stashing for the First $50
    1 Institutional Cookie Jars: Banks   3
    2 Credit Unions   13
    3 Uncle Sam and Savings Bonds   16

Part Two: The First $500
    4 Interest-Paying Checking Accounts   23
    5 Money Market Mutual Funds   26
    6 Bank Money Market Deposit Accounts   34
    7 Certificates of Deposit   38
    8 Mini-Investor Programs   43
    9 Investment Clubs   51

Part Three: The First $1,000
    10 Your IRA, Keogh, or SEP   57
    11 Your 401(k) Plan   69
    12 Treasuries for Ultrasafe Income   73

Part Four: The First $2,000
    13 Utilities and Hometown Companies   81
    14 Stocks and Ginnie Mae Mutual Funds   84
    15 Socially Conscious Mutual Funds   96
    16 Index Funds   99

Part Five: When You Have $5,000

17 Bonds: Corporates, Munis, and Zeros   107

18 A Stock Portfolio for Beginners   123

Part Six: Over the Top

19 REITs   137

20 Foreign Stocks and Bonds   139

21 Investing a Windfall   143

Appendix A: Nine Easy and Painless Ways to Save   149

Appendix B: Ten Steps Toward College Tuition   151

Appendix C: Scams, Swindles, and Suckers   155

Appendix D: The Top 25 Financial Websites   160

Appendix E: If You're Fired   167

Appendix F: Cash in a Flash: 10 Sources of Instant Money   173

Appendix G: Your Next Steps   180

Wall Street Jargon Made Simple   183

Index   189

Introduction

Getting the Most for Your Money

A fool and his money are soon parted.
   —English proverb

This book is intended to help you keep your money, whether you have just a few dollars or a few thousand. It seems as though most people, no matter how much money they make, really don't know how to save—or even if they do save, they don't know what to do with their savings. So, they and their money soon part ways.

Not a good thing.

This book is for you if . . .

- You're a new or small investor.
- You have money sitting in an account somewhere earning less than 3 percent interest.
- You're just starting out on your first job.
- You've saved several hundred dollars from your summer work.
- You have put aside several thousand dollars from careful budgeting.
- You received a sudden windfall so that for the first time in your life you have a lump sum to invest.
- You were handed a nice bonus at work.
- You have a business that's taking off.

So, no matter what your circumstances, I encourage you to start to save and invest right now—today. For the sooner you begin, the sooner your $50, $500, or $5,000 will grow and grow, so that eventually you can hand this book over to someone else.

Please don't wait until your next raise, until next year, or until next anything. Waiting means you'll never get started.

Never Too Little

Sometimes investors feel they don't have enough money to invest, that their options are limited. I'm here to tell you they're not. More than two dozen investment choices are described in this book.

You'll learn how to take advantage of each one. In fact, you'll soon discover that all the financial world is wooing you and your money: banks, brokerage firms, mutual fund companies, and financial planners are vying for your cash—be it $50 or $5,000.

Reaching Your Goals—How Saving Can Be Fun

Your personal financial goals will vary throughout your life, depending upon your age, your income, and your interests. The best way to reach any goal is to write it down, assign it a target date, and figure out how much you need to save to accomplish your dream. Here's a fill-in worksheet you can use as a model. Add your own particular spin to it.

Goal	Cost	Target Date	Months to Go	Save Each Month
Degree	$			$
Car	$			$
Computer	$			$
Vacation	$			$
House	$			$
New kitchen	$			$
Collectible	$			$
Start business	$			$

By the time you're halfway through this book, you'll be comfortable moving your money around from one investment to another as your needs change, as interest rates rise and fall, and as you earn more and more money.

Remember: The right place for your first $50 won't be the right one for your first $500 or $5,000—no one investment weathers all economic storms.

The Learning Process

Being a good investor does take some time and knowledge. If you follow my step-by-step plan—starting with $50—you'll soon know exactly what to do and when. I urge you to set aside some time to learn about handling your money, to explore the world of finance. Listen to the business news; read about it in newspapers, magazines, or online. Do so for one very simple reason: No one cares as much about your money as you do! No one.

Begin by checking out the box that follows called "The Ten Dumbest Mistakes People Make About Money." You'll soon see you're not alone in shying away from investing, in putting off saving.

Second, put a check mark next to those mistakes that are yours.

Third, reread my solutions for each mistake. They are simple and easy to follow.

Fourth and finally, resolve to take action today—or at least before the end of the month!

The Rule of 72

A quick way to calculate how long it will take you to double your investment—at any interest rate—is to use "The Rule of 72."

Divide 72 by the interest rate and you wind up with the number of years it will take to double your money.

For example:

72 divided by 3½ percent is 20½ years

72 divided by 6 percent is 12 years

Note: "The Rule of 72" applies only when interest and dividends are reinvested, and it does not take taxes into consideration.

The Ten Dumbest Mistakes People Make about Money

1. **Being Ashamed to Invest Small Amounts**. With this attitude, you'll never save anything. What is small to one investor may be huge to another. **Solution:** Begin saving something from your next income or salary check. The dollar amount is not important. Developing the habit of saving is. Then read Appendix A: "Nine Easy and Painless Ways to Save."

2. **Having Inadequate Emergency Savings**. Without this nest egg you could wind up deeply in debt. **Solution:** Stash three to six months' worth of living expenses in a money market fund or bank CD. (Read Chapters 5 and 7.)

3. **Leaving Cash in a Bank Savings Account**. The interest rate is far too low. **Solution:** Move it immediately to a money market fund or money market deposit account. (Read Chapters 5 and 6.)

4. **Operating Too Many Accounts**. If you have several bank accounts, a number of mutual funds, and brokerage accounts, you're spending too much on service fees. And it's way too difficult to keep track of rates, prices, and other details. **Solution:** Consolidate. Have one checking account, two or three mutual funds, and one brokerage account.

5. **Confusing Income with Appreciation.** If you don't know what an investment is for, you're likely to hold or sell the wrong thing. Do not expect growth stocks and growth mutual funds to

pay high dividends or income. Do not expect CDs, bonds, or utility stocks to rise in price. **Solution:** Read Chapters 17, 18, 19 and 20.

6. **Avoiding Financial Goal Setting**. Yogi Berra said it best: "If you don't know where you're going, you're probably going to wind up someplace else." Most people devote more time planning their vacations than their financial future. Consequently, they spend as much or more on cruises, airline tickets, and hotels than they do funding their retirement accounts or building up a nest egg. **Solution:** Set just one or two specific goals. Write them down or discuss them with a stockbroker or financial adviser. Ideally, do both.

7. **Failing to Diversify**. It's tempting to put all your money in one place because it's convenient and easy. No investment is ever sufficiently profitable or safe to justify this lazy approach. **Solution:** Divide your assets among CDs, money market funds, stocks, bonds, Treasuries, and real estate.

8. **Procrastinating**. Most of us put off making financial decisions because we're afraid we'll do the wrong thing. **Solution:** Set time deadlines and take several small, easy investment steps, one at a time. For example, if you have $3,000 on hand in week number one, put one-third into a money market fund. The next week, buy a bank CD. The following week, use the remaining amount to buy shares of a blue chip mutual fund.

9. **Ignoring Savings Plans at Work**. Tax-deferred 401(k) or stock purchase plans are good deals, especially if your company matches your contribution. So are automatic EE Savings Bond programs. **Solution:** Talk to your benefits officer this Monday, and read Appendix A: "Nine Easy and Painless Ways to Save."

10. **Failing to Have a Will**. If you care about the other people, in your life, keep an updated will. **Solution:** Call your lawyer this week.

Your Personal Financial Calendar

Copy and save this calendar and consult it year-round to avoid being hit with tax penalties, wasting your hard-earned money, and generally being financially foolish. *NOTE*: Tax dates are approximate and can change by a day or two depending whether or not they fall on a weekend or holiday.

January

- Do your annual Net Worth Statement.
- Determine your financial goals for the year; write them down.
- Set up file folders for your 1099s, W-2 form, tax-related documents; give up the old shoe box or shopping bag you've been using.
- Put business-related receipts in a separate folder; use them to document tax-deductible business expenses when you file next year's return. Include: receipts for taxis, tolls, gas, telephone and fax charges, rent, stationery, equipment, books, professional dues, etc. Read IRS publications #535, *Business Expenses* and #463, *Travel, Entertainment, Gift and Car Expenses*; both are free by calling 800-829-3676.
- Buy holiday cards and wrapping paper on sale. You'll save up to 75 percent.
- Pay off holiday credit card debt. Start with the card with the highest interest rate.

Tax Dates

- January 15. Your final estimated tax payment is due if you did not pay your income tax (or enough of your tax) for the year through withholding.

Use Form 1040ES

Personal Notes

_____

_____

_____

_____

_____

_____

February

• Call any banks, brokerage firms, mutual funds, or employers that have not sent you their IRS records by the end of the month.

• Make an appointment with your accountant to discuss taxes. The earlier, the less stressed out he/she will be and the more attention your return will receive.

• File income tax early and use any refund to reduce credit card debt and/or car or any other loan that doesn't have a prepayment penalty.

• Visit or call your local IRS office for copies of free booklets on preparing your tax return; avoid the March and April rush.

To order by phone, call: 800-829-3676 or download at: www.irs.gov

• Shop Presidents' Day sales for winter clothes.

• For a list of outlets in your area where prices are 25 to 70 percent less, call Outlet Bound, 800-336-8853 or log on to : www.outlet-bound.com.

• Get organized to swap your house or apartment for this summer's vacation and thus eliminate hotel bills. Contact: Homelink, 800-631-3841 or Intervac, 800-756-HOME.

• Book summer camps; good ones fill up early. Log on to the American Camping Association at: www.acacamps.org for a wealth of information.

Tax Dates

• February 15. If your child/student is working but will not earn enough to owe any tax, this is the last date to file a Form W-4 with his/her employer so that taxes will not be withheld.

Personal Notes

_____

_____

_____

March

• Challenge your property tax bill. Most states allow appeals in early spring. About half the home owners who question their assessments through official appeals win reductions of 10 percent. Read *How To Fight Property Taxes* from the National Taxpayers Union; $6.95; 703-683-5700.

• Finish preparing your tax return. If you're doing your own but need last-minute help, call the National Association of Enrolled Agents, 800-424-4339, for the names of those in your area; certified by the IRS, they are less expensive than CPAs.

• Buy air conditioners and fans before prices go up; you'll save anywhere from $50 to $250 per appliance.

• Confirm that colleges have received your financial aid forms. Deadline for the Free Application for Federal Student Aid (FAFSA) varies.

Personal Notes

_____

_____

_____

_____

_____

_____

_____

_____

April

- Move this month if it's part of your plan; costs are 40 to 50 percent less between October 1 and May 1 and highest during the summer months when kids are out of school. Save all receipts if your move is job related; some expenses may be deductible.

> Read IRS publication #521, *Moving Expenses*; free
> by calling 800-829-3676

- Support Earth Day, April 22. Reduce cost of garbage pickup and recycling by contacting Mail Preference Service Direct Marketing Association, 212-768-7277. They will remove your name from mailing lists. To get off all lists, consult *Stop Junk Mail Forever*, $4.50 from: Good Advice Press, 845-758-1400.

Tax Dates

- April 15. File your income tax return.
- April 15. This is the last day you can fund your IRA.
- April 15. Fund your Keogh or SEP if you have self-employment income.
- April 15. If you are not filing your taxes, get an automatic four-month extension by filing Form 4868. And pay any tax you estimate will be due. An extension applies to the filing time but not to the time for paying taxes due. You will be penalized if the total tax you've paid including withholding and estimated payments does not equal at least 90 percent of the tax you owe.

  NOTE: If you get an extension, you cannot file Form 1040EZ.

- April 15. Pay the first quarterly installment of your estimated taxes if you're not paying income tax through withholdings.
- April 15. Pay your IRA trustee or custodial fee with a separate check so it is tax deductible.
- Call 800-829-1040 for last-minute filing help. To hear recorded tax info on 150-plus topics, call TeleTax at 800-829-4477.

Personal Notes

_____

_____

May

• Get your air conditioner overhauled; clean and/or replace the filter to increase efficiency.

• Make spring cleaning pay off. If your power company has two-tier pricing, wash and dry your curtains, bedspreads, and cotton rugs in the evening when rates are lower. Ditto on washing dishes.

• Do some financial spring cleaning. Take an inventory of your household possessions and check insurance coverage. Items should be covered at their replacement value, not what they initially cost. Videotape your possessions; for jewelry, antiques, collectibles, furs, and other valuables, get an appraisal. For the name of a local appraiser, call the American Society of Appraisers, 703-748-2228 or log on to: www.appraisers.org.

☞ **Tip**: Keep a copy of your inventory at work or in your safe deposit box.

• Book summer vacation hotel, resort, and airline tickets now to avoid last-minute, outrageously high rates. For the best deals, including packages, check with Travel Smart, 800-FARE-OFF or www.TravelSmartNews.com.

• Cut vacation costs by reserving space early in a national park. Call the National Park Reservation System, 800-365-2267 or reservations.nps.gov.

• Check your frequent flier miles now and use them to get space on planes for the summer months.

• Call the IRS if you haven't received your tax refund: 800-829-1040.

Personal Notes

_____

_____

_____

June

- Do a semiannual review of your investments. Note the total return figures and yields and compare them with those of January 1 and of one year ago. Then . . .

- Meet with your stockbroker or financial adviser to review your account. Decide what securities to sell or to hold.

- Give a garage or yard sale. Invest the cash you take in.

- Donate what you don't sell to charity for a tax deduction. Get a receipt.

> Read IRS Publication #526, *Charitable Contributions*;
> 800-829-3676 or www.irs.gov.

- Rent, don't buy, wedding dress, bridesmaid clothes, and tuxedos; you'll save at least 50 percent.

- Get a tune-up for your car; check air-conditioning, water, coolant, and tires, especially if you're going on a driving trip.

- Find a last-minute summer job at: www.summerjobs.com.

- Pay down your credit card debt so you don't run short on your vacation.

Tax Dates

- June 15. Pay the second installment of your estimated tax.

- June 30. If you have a bank, securities, or other financial account in a foreign country worth more than $10,000, you must file Form TDF 90-22-1 with the Department of Treasury by this date.

Personal Notes

_____

_____

_____

_____

_____

July

- Read a good investment book while at the beach or lake.

  🖝 **Tip:** Keep the receipt; it may be tax deductible.

- Talk with colleagues or friends about starting an investment club in the fall. During the summer, read the information published by the National Association of Investment Clubs (NAIC), 877-275-6242.

- Track your cash flow during this lazy month. Then resolve to cut back on unnecessary and impulsive purchases come September 1.

- Sell your old car. Now through September, the market is better than usual as college students and high school seniors need cars for summer jobs and to return to school.

Personal Notes

_____

_____

_____

_____

_____

_____

_____

_____

_____

_____

August

- Go for good deals on lawn and patio furniture, bathing suits, lawn mowers, barbecue grills, camping gear, and ski equipment.
- Prepare your child or grandchild for going off to college. Discuss checking accounts, credit cards, and do a joint budget for the school year.
- Visit a stock exchange or Federal Reserve Bank or branch while traveling in the U.S. or abroad. Most have excellent tours and gift shops.
- Check with your accountant: Travel that combines work and play may be partially deductible, provided the primary purpose is business.

Tax Dates

- August 15. If you filed for a four-month extension, your income tax return is now due.
- August 15. Last date to file for a further two-month extension.

Personal Notes

_____

_____

_____

_____

_____

_____

_____

_____

September

- Go back to school. Take a class in financial planning, investing, or money management.
- Figure out what your child earned from a summer job. Ask your accountant if he/she needs to file a tax return.

> Read: IRS Publication #4, *Student's Guide to Federal Income Tax*; free at 800-829-3676.

- Weatherize your home. Call your local power company for a free (or inexpensive) energy audit.
- Shop the sales: Skis, snowboarding equipment, car batteries, and paint are traditionally on sale.

Tax Dates

- September 15. Pay the third installment of your quarterly estimated tax.

Personal Notes

_____

_____

_____

_____

_____

_____

_____

_____

October

- Review your will. Since this is a slow month regarding taxes, use the time to reread or write your will. Update your will if you've gotten married, separated, or divorced; if you've had a child or grandchild; if your income has changed significantly; if you've moved to a new state; if a close relative or someone named in your will has died; if the tax laws have changed.

- Service your furnace. Replace disposable filters or clean permanent ones.

- Caulk around windows and doors to reduce heating costs.

- Get your flu shot or checkup before cold season sets in. Good health is one way to cut medical costs. Buy prescription drugs at a discount through a mail order pharmacy such as the one operated by the American Association of Retired Persons.

☞ **Tip**: You don't have to be retired or a member to participate. Call: 800-456-2277 for prices.

Tax Dates

- October 15. If you received both a four-month and an additional two-month extension for your tax return, file now and pay any tax, interest, and penalties due.

- October 15. This is the last day to make a Keogh or SEP contribution if you were granted an extension.

Personal Notes

_____

_____

_____

_____

_____

_____

November

• Talk with your broker about securities you may wish to sell before the year's end.

• Make charitable donations for tax deduction.

• To find out if a charity is approved for tax purposes, get in touch with the National Charities Information Bureau, 212-929-6300 or www.ncib.org

☞ **Tip**: If your gift is more than $250, a canceled check is not adequate proof for the IRS. You must have a written acknowledgment of your donation from the charity to be able to deduct it. If your gift is property, not cash, the letter must include a description of the property.

• Buy a car this month. Dealers, forced to clear their showrooms for next year's models, start reducing prices and offering rebates and good financing deals.

• Quit smoking during the American Cancer Society's "Great American Smokeout Week," held this month. At $3.50 a pack, one pack a day is $1,277.50 a year. Put that amount into your IRA. You'll also cut the cost of your health insurance premiums.

• Start making Christmas and Hanukkah cards and gifts.

• Get free firewood. If you live near one of the 155 national forests, you may be able to pick up several cords of firewood for free or for a small fee. (A cord of wood regularly runs $85 to $125, depending upon where you live.) Check with your regional office of the U.S. Forest Service or call the Federal Information.

• Make sure you spend all the money in your Flexible Spending Account before December 31. Any left goes to your employer, not you!

Personal Notes

_____

_____

_____

December

• Empty closets and cupboards and give away items to charity for an end-of-the-year tax deduction.

• Review last year's tax return; it will remind you of the tax-deductible expenses you took and can probably take again.

• Play Santa Claus. You can give up to $10,000 to any number of people and not pay a gift tax. Checks should be cashed before the end of the year.

• Push investment income, bonuses, and freelance earnings into next year to delay paying income taxes; you'll also have use of the money for a year.

Tax Dates

• December 31 is the last day to set up a Keogh Plan for next year. You have until April 15 to fund it, but you must do the official paperwork now.

• December 31. This is the last day to pay deductible items, such as state estimated taxes, and still get a deduction.

Personal Notes

_____

_____

_____

_____

_____

_____

_____

PART ONE

SAFE STASHING FOR THE FIRST $50

1
Institutional Cookie Jars: Banks

"That's where the money is," Willie Sutton told a reporter when asked why he robbed banks.

Some of your money should be in one too. And for that first $50, a bank savings account is the most logical place to begin.

Selecting a Bank

Like Willie, you want the best bank possible for your $50. However, not all banks treat all customers equally. So don't make a mad dash to the bank on the corner. It pays to shop around, even with only $50 burning a hole in your pocket. Eventually you will become a larger depositor and will need to use the bank for other reasons—a loan, a mortgage, or a checking account, certified checks, even references.

Since most Americans are always in a hurry, the single most common factor in deciding where to bank is, of course, location. Yet your nearest bank is not necessarily the right choice.

Before opening a savings account, check out your neighborhood bank, by all means, but also make personal visits to several others.

At each one make an appointment with the person in charge of new accounts. Describe your financial needs; pay attention to what this person suggests. Don't worry about the quality of the wall-to-wall carpeting or the abundance of fresh flowers. Decor is not the issue, but other things certainly are.

Check to see:

- What the minimum deposit requirement is for a savings account.
- If all types of services are offered.
- How well rush-hour traffic is handled.
- If there are express lines.
- If there are branches near both where you live and where you work.
- If there are bank officers available to answer questions, or if you are likely to be sent scurrying from one desk to another, in a Kafka-like circle.
- If there is written material available on interest rates and service charges—material that you can actually understand.
- Then, compare fees and interest rates of all the banks you visit.

And check out **credit unions**.

Credit unions emerged in this country in the early 1900s to help those working-class people who didn't qualify for loans from commercial banks. The members of a credit union pooled their money and made low-interest loans to one another. Today credit unions serve groups of people with a common bond (see Chapter 2 for more on these institutions).

Although banks are free to pay whatever rate they choose, as of mid-2002 they were paying 0.6–2.8 percent on savings accounts while credit unions were averaging 2–4.5 percent. Web-only banks have even higher rates. That should tell you something.

The stated rate, however, is only the tip of the iceberg. It is also important to know exactly how often the interest will be paid, because every time your account is credited with interest, you'll earn interest on that interest, which is known as **compounding**.

So open your account at a bank where interest is compounded daily, not quarterly. You'll make more money.

Fees

In many banks, if your balance falls below a certain amount, you will be assessed a monthly charge or you will lose interest, or possibly both.

Or, if your account is inactive, meaning you have not made a deposit or withdrawal during a certain time period, banks typically charge a small monthly fee.

Yield

Banks often advertise two figures: the annual interest rate and the **effective yield**. The difference between the two depends on how often interest is credited to your balance, thus increasing the principal on which interest is paid. A 3 percent interest rate has an effective annual yield of 3 percent if the interest is credited annually. If it is credited quarterly, the effective yield is 3.094 percent, and if interest is credited monthly, the effective yield is 3.116 percent.

Internet or Virtual Banks

Many of the best rates on loans and savings are available at banks that operate via the Internet, rather than at traditional brick-and-mortar institutions. Because they have lower operating costs, these "virtual" banks are also much more likely to have low (or no) fees or minimum deposits.

Internet Banks

FOR WHOM
- Depositors who are comfortable managing their money online.

Where to Find
- The Internet (see list below)

Minimum
- Determined by individual banks. Many have no minimum; others start at as low as $50 or $100.

Safety
- These banks take extensive security precautions to protect depositors.
- High, if FDIC insured.

Advantages
- High rates on accounts.
- Low (or no) fees or minimums.
- Convenience of 24-hour access to your account.

Disadvantages
- Must be comfortable with Internet navigation.
- Takes longer to open an account; anywhere from a few days to a few weeks.
- More expensive for frequent ATM users. Many local banks don't charge customers a surcharge for use of their own ATMs. However, "web-only" banks have no ATMs of their own, so customers typically pay a fee for ATM access to their account. Although some web banks rebate up to $6 a month in fees, this may not cover your monthly usage.

Leading Internet Banks
- First Internet Bank
  www.firstib.com 888-873-3424

- ING Direct
  www.ingdirect.com 800-ING-DIRECT

- Lighthousebank
  www.lighthousebank.com 877-668-2265

- NetBank
  www.netbank.com 888-256-6932

- Security First Network Bank
  www.sfnb.com 800-736-2322

Coupon Clubs

It's certainly gimmicky, but if it helps you save, then give the bank coupon club a try.

The coupon club is the generic name for a myriad of programs devised by banks to attract business. These include Christmas clubs, Hanukkah clubs, and vacation clubs. They are also offered by many savings and loan associations and credit unions.

Coupon Clubs

FOR WHOM
- Undisciplined savers.
- People with large families who have to buy lots of holiday gifts.
- Those who like tearing along perforated lines.

FEE
- Usually none.

SAFETY
- High.

ADVANTAGES
- Forced way to save.

- Some clubs pay low interest or no interest at all.
- Some pay interest only if you complete the full term of the club.
- You may not be able to withdraw your money until the full term is over.

If you decide to join one, each week or month, depending upon the club, you make a specified deposit or payment, enclosing a coupon with your money. At the end of a stated period, usually a year, your coupons will all be gone and your account full of money. In some clubs you cannot withdraw your money until the stated period is over. Ask.

Couponless Plans

In many banks, you can sign up for automatic savings deposit plans. You designate the monthly amount you want to save, say $35. This amount is then automatically taken out of your checking account and deposited into your savings account, where it will earn interest. The record of your transaction is then attached to your monthly checking account statement.

$50 Compounded at 5 Percent

COMPOUNDING PERIODS PER YEAR

Years	Annually	Semiannually	Quarterly	Monthly	Daily
1	$52.50	$52.53	$52.55	$52.56	$52.58
2	63.81	64.00	64.10	64.17	64.20
10	81.44	81.93	82.18	82.35	83.43
20	132.66	134.25	135.07	135.63	135.90

(Source: Credit Union National Association, Inc.)

ATMs

Automated teller machines, electronic machines located on just about every corner of America, provide instant access to money 24 hours a day. To use an ATM you need an encoded plastic card issued by the bank, which is inserted into the machine, and a personal identification number (PIN). This PIN number is then punched in on the machine to access your account. Obviously you should never give your PIN number to another person nor have it written down in your wallet; instead pick a number that you can memorize, such as your wedding anniversary or your mother's birthday.

🖑 **Caution** Don't pick your own birthday—thieves are on to that one.

Although ATMs are a godsend on weekends and when bank lines are long, use them with discretion:

- Check to see whether your bank charges for ATM transactions when you use its own ATM; if so, pick a different bank.
- Very often cards issued by one bank may be used in the ATM of another bank, but for a fee. Find out.
- Use a bank that is part of an ATM network, such as PLUS, MAC, MOST, NYCE, SAM, STAR, or Cirrus, in which case you can use your ATM when you're out of state or even overseas.
- Visa, MasterCard, and American Express can be used in many ATMs for cash advances. Check the fee for doing so.

🖑 **Caution** On credit card advances you often pay service charges as well as interest beginning from the minute you receive the cash.

- Time your withdrawals. If you want money from your bank's money market deposit account where it's earning interest, make your withdrawal by ATM after 3 P.M., the bank's official closing hour. That way you'll get the maximum interest.

🔆 **Hint** Each bank sets a limit on how much cash you can withdraw on any one day. If you're planning to get cash for a trip, check the daily limit first.

Ways to Get the Most out of Your Bank

New electronic systems, revised banking rules, and expanded marketing programs all mean better deals for savvy bank customers.
Read the examples below and then talk to your banker. These and
other "deals" are not always advertised.

- *Currency exchange.* When abroad, get an exchange rate bar-
  gain by using a bank's automated teller machine (ATM) card to
  purchase foreign currency. Your PLUS or CIRRUS card, issued
  by U.S. banks that are members of one of these ATM networks,
  may be used at thousands of outlets around the world to withdraw local currency. The machine dispenses currency at an
  exchange rate that's several percentage points less than the
  official retail rate. And you don't pay the added transaction
  cost that many banks, hotels, and others charge for accepting
  U.S. dollar traveler's checks.
- *Senior citizens' programs.* Free checking, no-fee credit cards,
  free traveler's checks, and discounts on tickets to cultural
  events for customers over age fifty.
- *Favorable loan and mortgage rates.* Banks often give preferential
  treatment to customers when it comes to lending money. Ask.
- *Fees waived.* Customers who combine deposits and loans and
  keep a minimum balance don't always have to pay service
  charges.

A Bank Checkup

- Ask your banker how interest is compounded.
- Get a printed chart of interest rates to study at home.
- Ask if the bank pays interest only on the lowest balance during
  the quarter. For example, if you have $200 in your account and
  you take out $75, then eventually build it back up to $200, is
  interest paid as though you had only $125 in the account all
  the time?
- Look for a bank paying interest from day of deposit to day of
  withdrawal.

- Will you be charged extra if you make many withdrawals?
- Are there any days at the end of the quarter when interest is not paid?
- How many days are counted in the bank's year? (Some banks have "dead days" at the end of a quarter when they don't pay interest.)
- If you take out money or close the account at midquarter, will you lose interest?
- Are there penalties for leaving your account inactive for a long period?
- Is there a monthly service charge?

Study the chart on annually compounded interest in a $50 account and use it as a guideline for making your banking decision.

How Safe Is Your Bank?

Although occasionally banks fail, that's no reason to tuck your money under the mattress. But you should:
- Bank only at federally insured institutions. Look for the FDIC sign at the bank. It stands for Federal Deposit Insurance Corporation, an independent agency of the U.S. government that was established by Congress in 1933 to insure bank deposits. Member banks pay for the cost of insurance through semi-annual assessments.
- Keep in mind that individual depositors, not accounts, are insured—up to $100,000, including interest and principal. That means if you have two accounts in the same name in one bank, you are insured for only $100,000, not $200,000.
- Find out how safe your bank really is. For a small fee, Veribanc, Inc., will send you a financial evaluation of any bank or savings and loan as well as its FDIC category—well capitalized, adequately capitalized, or undercapitalized. Contact: Veribanc, Inc., P.O. Box 461, Wakefield, MA 01880; 800-442-2657; 781-245-8370, or www.veribanc.com.
- If you discover that your bank is a weakling, move your money

to the strongest institution in your area. Veribanc will provide the names of such banks for a fee.

🔆 **Hint** You may wish to wait until any certificates of deposit mature before transferring money so as not to lose out on any interest.

- For a free copy of *Your Insured Deposit*, log on to: www.fdic.gov.
- Bank accounts that you manage for someone else, such as a custodian account for a child or parent, do not count toward the cap on your personal FDIC insurance coverage. For full details on coverage, go to: www.fdic.gov and click on "Are My Bank Accounts Insured?"
- For more information on FDIC insurance call the consumer hotline at: 877-ASK-FDIC. Also ask for a free copy of *Your Insured Deposit*.

2 Credit Unions

Once thought of only as a place for assembly-line workers to get a car loan, credit unions are much sought after today by anyone who can become a member. They are an excellent choice for your first $50, and they inevitably pay one or two percentage points above bank rates. There is no lid on interest rates; they vary from union to union.

Credit unions are cooperatives, or not-for-profit associations of people who pool their savings and then lend money to one another. By law, they must have a so-called common bond, which may consist in working for the same employer, belonging to the same church, club, or government agency, or even living in the same neighborhood. Because they are not-for-profits and because overhead costs are low, credit unions almost always give savers and borrowers better rates and terms than commercial institutions.

Theoretically, unions are run by the depositors—every member, in fact, must be a depositor, albeit a very small one. The true organizational work, however, is done by volunteer committees in the smaller unions and by paid employees in the larger ones.

Credit Unions

For Whom
- Members and members' families.

Where to Find
- Your place of work.
- Your neighborhood association.
- Church, club, synagogue, YMCA, YWCA.

Minimum
- You must buy at least one share to join a credit union.
- Shares are determined by each union and vary from $5–$30, with most around $15. (A share is really your first deposit.)

Safety
- Varies, but generally above average.
- High if insured by National Credit Union Share Insurance Fund.

Advantages
- Friendly, supportive attitude toward members.
- Interest rates on savings are generally higher than at commercial institutions.
- Interest rates on loans are generally lower than at commercial institutions.
- Other services may be offered, such as mortgages, credit cards, checking accounts, IRAs, CDs.
- An automatic payroll deduction savings plan is frequently available.

Disadvantages
- Might be run by inexperienced volunteers or inadequately staffed.
- Might not be adequately insured.
- May not return canceled checks.

☀️ **Hint:** If you are not a member of a credit union but would like to be one, call the industry's trade organization for information on how to join or start one: 800-358-5710 or log on to: www.cuna.org.

Before you invest your $50 in a credit union:

- Make sure the credit union is insured by the National Credit Union Administration, a federal agency.
- Check it out by calling the agency at: 703-518-6300 or log on to: www.ncua.gov.

Uncle Sam and Savings Bonds

The bank isn't the only safe place for your $50. Uncle Sam is willing and eager to keep it for you and, in return, provide a little something in the way of interest through what is known as a U.S. savings bond. (When you buy a U.S. savings bond you are lending money to the U.S. government.)

Series EE Savings Bonds are an easy way to save small amounts of money (known as preserving capital) and at the same time earn interest.

You can buy EE bonds at most banks and there's no fee. The purchase price is actually 50 percent of the bond's face value, so in other words, a $50 bond costs only $25. (EE savings bonds are sold in the following face value amounts: $50, $75, $100, $200, $500, $1,000, $5,000, and $10,000.)

If you hold them until maturity, you'll get back the face value, $50 in the case of a $25 bond. In other words, both the principal (the $25 in this example) and interest are paid in a lump sum when the bond is redeemed at maturity.

Interest rates vary depending on when a bond is purchased and how long it is held. If bonds earn an average of 4 percent per year, the full face value will be reached in 18 years; at 6 percent, in 12 years.

One of the great pluses to EE bonds: The interest you earn is exempt from state and local income taxes and personal property taxes. You do, however, have to pay federal income, gift, and estate taxes.

☀ **Hint** There is, however, a way to avoid federal income tax that is related to using the bonds for college tuition. See Appendix B, "Ten Steps Toward College Tuition," for full details.

In addition, you have the option of not reporting the federal income tax until you redeem the bonds, or you can report the interest every year as it accrues. Check with your accountant.

EE Bonds issued on or after May 1, 1997, earn interest based on the yield on Treasury securities. Interest is added every six months to the redemption value of the bond rather than being paid out to you, the bondholder. That's a real plus: You won't be able to spend the interest.

✋ **Caution** Bonds stop earning interest at final maturity date, and at that point, they should be redeemed or rolled over into Series HH Bonds. HH Bonds earn a flat 4 percent.

Inflation-Indexed Bonds

In September 1998, the Treasury began selling savings bonds with interest rates adjusted for inflation. I-bonds, as they're called, come with a guarantee that your return will outpace inflation. Of course, this will only be appealing if we experience inflation.

Interest on the I-bond equals the inflation rate plus a fixed rate of return, which as we go to press is 5.92 percent. Once you buy an I-bond, the fixed rate stays the same until the bond stops earning interest after 30 years. The interest rate changes every May and November, based on the current inflation rate.

At Work

In addition to buying these bonds at a bank or credit union, you may also buy them through an automatic payroll deduction plan, called the **EasySaver Program**—provided your employer participates. This is a great way to stockpile small dollar amounts, especially if you're not a natural saver. In fact, after a while you won't even miss the amount taken from your payroll. **Details**: 877-811-SAVE and www.savingsbonds.gov.

☼ **Hint** For the current rate on savings bonds, call: 800-US-BONDS or log on to: www.savingsbonds.gov. The rate changes each November 1 and May 1.

EE Savings Bonds

FOR WHOM
- Those who can wait ten or more years for their return.
- Those who have a low tolerance for risk and want to be certain that their principal is safe.

WHERE TO PURCHASE
- Banks.
- Payroll savings plan.
- Credit unions.
- Online at: www.savingsbonds.gov
- By preauthorized debits to your bank account.

FEE AND MINIMUM
- No fee.
- Minimum purchase: $25 for a $50 bond.

SAFETY RATING
- Highest possible.

ADVANTAGES
- Virtually no risk because the principal is backed by the U.S. government.
- Interest is guaranteed.
- Easy to buy at your local bank.

- No commission or sales fee.
- Income is exempt from state and local taxes.
- Federal tax can be deferred until bonds are redeemed or mature.
- EE bonds are an excellent way to save for a child's education, especially if you can target them to come due after he or she reaches age 14, at which point the interest income will be taxed at the child's lower rate. (Until the child turns 14, however, earned investment income from assets in a child's name are taxed at the parent's presumably higher rate.)
- EE bonds purchased after January 1, 1990 by someone at least age 24 and used to pay college tuition are free from federal income tax provided you fall within certain income guidelines when the bonds are redeemed. Ask your local bank for details.
- Upon maturity, you may reinvest—roll over—your Series EE Savings Bonds into Series HH bonds and further defer your taxes until the HH bonds mature, another ten years down the road. HH bonds can be purchased only by rolling over EE bonds that have reached maturity and are available in denominations of $500, $1,000, $5,000, and $10,000.

☼ **Hint** For the current rate on bonds, telephone: 800-US-BONDS or log on to: www.savingsbonds.gov.
　🖐 **Help!**
- These publications are free from:
  Bureau of Public Debt
  200 Third Street
  Parkersburg, VA 26106
  Investor Information Guide
  Questions and Answers on the Education Bond Program
  Guaranteed Minimum Rate Charts

- For information on payroll savings plans, call: 304-480-6112 or log on to: www.savingsbonds.gov
- For information on the EasySaver Plan, call: 877-811-7283 or log on to: www.savingsbonds.gov
- Get the free IRS Publication #550, *Investment Income and Expenses* by calling: 800-829-3676.

PART TWO

THE FIRST $500

4
Interest-Paying Checking Accounts

It's a good idea to keep in mind that holding cash is actually an investment choice—there are a number of places where you can park $500 or more, earn interest, and have fairly easy access to your money. We will discuss the five best in the pages that follow. They are:

- Interest-paying checking accounts.
- Money market mutual funds.
- Insured bank money market deposit accounts.
- Bank certificates of deposit (CDs).
- Treasury bills, notes, and bonds.

Note: Savings accounts and EE savings bonds are two other choices, available for less than $500; they were described in Part One.

First, let's take a look at interest-paying checking accounts, sometimes called NOW accounts. NOW stands for Negotiable Order of Withdrawal. These are like regular checking accounts with printed checks and statements, but the good part is they also pay interest—anywhere from 1.25 percent to 3 percent.

Interest-Paying Checking Accounts

FOR WHOM
- Ideal for anyone who wants a checking account and can maintain the bank's minimum balance at all times.

MINIMUM
- Varies from around $500 to $2,500 or more.

SAFETY FACTOR
- FDIC-insured, up to $100,000.

ADVANTAGES
- You earn interest on a checking account.
- You can write checks for any dollar amount.
- You may get overdraft privileges so checks don't bounce.

DISADVANTAGES
- Bank charges on regular checking accounts are almost universally lower than on these interest-paying accounts.
- Minimums for maintaining accounts are steep.

Use them as a handy housekeeping account where you can earn a little interest on your cash balance as you pay your bills.

There's one real drawback attached to these NOW accounts: In order to earn the interest, you must maintain a minimum or a monthly average balance. Find out what it is. Minimums vary nationwide from about $500 to $2,500 or sometimes higher.

🖐 **Caution** If you fall below the required minimum balance, you will lose interest and you may also be subject to per-check, per-deposit, and/or monthly charges.

The equivalent of this account at a credit union is called a share draft. Since credit unions don't have a cap on the amount of interest they can pay, share drafts generally offer slightly higher rates than bank accounts. (**See** Chapter 2 for more on credit unions.)

✐ **Tip**: In today's competitive banking world, an interest-paying checking account is a good choice if you can maintain the minimum amount in order to avoid any steep fees and charges—these eat up any earned interest. Take time to do your calculations carefully. If you know it will be difficult for you to maintain the minimum balance, open a regular checking account instead.

Money Market Mutual Funds

After you've opened a checking account and accumulated an extra $500, your next step is to find a safe place to put your hard-earned savings. One of the best and safest choices is a money market mutual fund where you'll earn considerably more interest than in a regular savings or NOW account.

What Is a Mutual Fund?

To understand what a money market mutual fund is, you first need to know how mutual funds in general work.

A mutual fund is actually an investment company in which you (i.e., the public) buy shares. This means your investment dollars are pooled with those of thousands of other investors and the combined total is invested by a professional manager in various things—stocks, bonds, Treasuries, CDs, etc.

The fund manager studies the market, interest rates, and other economic indicators, buying and selling those investments that best suit the fund's stated aim or goal. A fund's goal might be to achieve income, price appreciation, or tax-free returns for its shareholders.

The Top Yielding Money Market Funds

Fund	Telephone	Web Addresses	Minimum
Dreyfus Basic	800-645-6561	www.dreyfus.com	$25,000
Fidelity Spartan	800-544-8888	www.fidelity.com	20,000
Fidelity Cash Reserves	800-544-8888	www.fidelity.com	2,500
Dreyfus World- wide Dollar	800-645-6561	www.dreyfus.com	2,500
Strong Investors Fund	800-368-1030	www.strong.com	1,000
Alger Portfolio	800-992-3863	www.algerfunds.com	500

The Powerful Advantages of Mutual Funds

The value of a fund is that one large pool of money can be far more effectively invested than hundreds or thousands of small sums. Each investor in a fund, no matter how large or small his or her investment, then owns a proportional share of what the fund owns, and receives a proportional return, without discrimination based on the number of shares he or she owns.

Types of Funds

There are many types of funds. Some are set up for long-term growth, some for immediate income, others for tax-free returns. Some take higher risks than others. Some are devoted exclusively to buying and selling stocks; others to bonds; and some, to a combination of the two.

What's in a Money Market Fund?

In the case of a money market fund, the goal is a high yield with minimum risk. Money market funds derive their name from the type of securities they invest in: "money market" securities.

Financial companies, large corporations, and the U.S. government all borrow large sums of money for short periods of time by issuing (or selling) money market securities in exchange for cash. (Short periods of time means one year or less.)

What Kinds of Things Money Market Funds Buy

Agency securities. Issued by government agencies such as the Government National Mortgage Association (Ginnie Mae) and the Small Business Administration or by government-sponsored organizations such as the Federal National Mortgage Association (Fannie Mae) and the Federal Home Loan Banks.

Bankers' acceptances. Commercial notes guaranteed by a bank.

Certificates of deposit. Large-denomination negotiable CDs sold by both U.S. and foreign commercial banks. When over $100,000, they are known as "jumbo CDs."

Treasury bills and notes. Sold on a periodic basis by the U.S. Treasury and backed by the "full faith and credit" of the government.

Repurchase agreements. "Repros" are buy-sell deals in which the mutual fund buys securities with an agreement that the seller will actually repurchase them within a short time—generally seven days or less—at a price that includes interest for that time. The fund holds the securities as collateral.

Yankee CDs. Certificates issued by U.S. branches of foreign banks.

For example, the government borrows by way of selling Treasury bills, notes, and bonds. Large corporations do so by issuing IOUs called commercial paper, and banks by way of large certificates of deposit, called jumbo CDs.

These money market securities make up the fund's portfolio, rather than stocks and bonds.

The borrowers—the government, large corporations, and banks—are all good credit risks. They consist of the country's most solid institutions and they all agree to pay back the money quickly and at high interest rates. That's why you can earn more in a money market fund than in a traditional savings account.

Obviously, no ordinary saver would be able to participate in this venture on his or her own. The amounts involved are simply too large. Yet through a money market mutual fund, you, the average investor, can indeed share in this opportunity, safely and cheaply. The money earned by the fund after expenses is in turn paid out to you, the shareholder, as interest or "dividends."

Picking the Best Money Market Fund

STEP 1. Although many funds require a minimum deposit of $1,000 or $2,000 just to open an account, there is one fund with no minimum opening requirement (or $500 if you want checks). It's a good place to begin. Call and get a copy of the prospectus and account application:

Alger Money Market Portfolio
800-992-3863

With a money market fund, you have what's known as liquidity— you have immediate access to your money without any penalty. You can cash in your shares by phone, mail, or through your broker if you have a brokerage-sponsored fund. And funds will wire money directly into your local bank if you so arrange in advance.

You can also tap your money by writing checks against your shares. Usually a fund permits unlimited check writing just as long as the checks are for amounts over $500. And the nice thing about it is, the checks are free.

STEP 2. If you want a fund that will let you write checks for any amount, look into these two; they have an opening minimum of $1,500:

- Federated Money Market Management
- Liberty U.S. Government Money Market Fund

Both are part of the hugely successful mutual fund company Federated Investors in Pittsburgh, PA (800-245-0242).

Many money market funds will waive their opening minimum if you sign up for their automatic savings plan. In some cases, there's no opening minimum. *Ask.* In this type of plan, you agree to invest a certain amount, usually $50, a month, which is taken automatically from your checking account and wired into your money market fund.

Safety

How safe are money market funds? Although they are not federally insured, they are considered very, very safe. Since they were launched in the early seventies, only two out of hundreds have run into trouble. Back in 1979, First Multifund of New York, which was paying an extremely high rate—93 cents on the dollar—closed its doors. More recently, Community Bankers U.S. Government Money Market Fund was forced to liquidate owing to risky derivative investments.

The reason money market funds are considered so safe is that regulations require that only 5 percent of a fund's assets may be held in the obligations of any one institution other than the obligations of the U.S. government.

♀ **Hint** The safest funds of all, of course, are those that invest only in U.S. guaranteed securities. You will certainly sacrifice a point or two in exchange for safety, but do so if it means you'll sleep better. Among those to consider are:

- Capital Preservation Fund
  www.American Century.com
  800-345-2021

- Fidelity U.S. Government Reserves
  www.Fidelity.com
  800-544-8888
- T. Rowe Price U.S. Treasury Money Market Fund
  www.Troweprice.com
  800-638-5660
- Vanguard Money Market Reserves Treasury Portfolio
  www.Vanguard.com
  800-662-7447

Tax-Exempt Money Funds

The dividends you earn on most funds are fully taxable. Yet there are some funds that invest solely in tax-exempt securities—and their dividends are not taxed by the IRS at the federal level, only at the state and local levels.

✋ **Caution** Unless you're in a high tax bracket, it doesn't pay to buy into a tax-exempt fund because their yields are considerably lower than those paid by taxable money market funds (see page 32).

🔅 **Hint** However, for the day when your taxable income puts you in a high tax bracket, you will want to consider investing in a tax-free money market fund. Two of the best:
- Dreyfus Tax-Exempt Money Market Fund
  800-645-6561
  www.dreyfus.com
- Franklin/Templeton Tax-Exempt Money Market Fund
  800-237-0738
  www.franklintempleton.com

Double and Triple Tax-Exempt Money Funds

If you live in a state with high income tax rates, you can get an even bigger tax break from a fund in which the interest earned is free of state and federal income taxes and, in many cases, from local taxes. A list regularly appears in the financial pages of major newspapers, in *The Wall Street Journal, Barron's,* and popular money magazines, such as *Money.*

Among the states with particularly high taxes: New York, California, Minnesota, Michigan, Massachusetts, New Jersey, Pennsylvania, and probably yours!

Call these mutual fund companies and ask if they have such a fund for the state in which you live:

Calvert: 800-368-2745
Dreyfus: 800-645-6561
Fidelity: 800-544-8888
Franklin: 800-237-0738
Lexington: 800-526-0056
T. Rowe Price: 800-638-5660
Vanguard: 800-662-7447

Help! This service provides continually updated professional and safety ratings for money market mutual funds. Call or write for a complimentary copy:

The Money Letter (bimonthly; $99)
Agora Financial Publishing
360 Holliston Street, Box 6020
Holliston, MA 01746
800-890-9670
www.moneyletter.com

Should You Buy a Tax-Exempt Fund?

To determine if a tax-exempt fund is worthwhile:

1. Subtract your tax bracket (28 percent in this example), from the number 1.

1 minus .28 = .72

2. Then, divide the tax-free yield the fund is paying by .72 to find the taxable equivalent.

3. The result is the yield you'd need on a taxable investment

to match the tax-free yield. For example, if a tax-free investment is yielding 5.5 percent, divide 5.5 by .72. The result, 7.64, is the yield you'd need to beat with a taxable investment if you're in the 28 percent tax bracket.

6 Bank Money Market Deposit Accounts

Top-notch protection and liquidity. This almost unbeatable combination is available when you open a money market deposit account (MMDA) at your bank. These accounts are insured for up to $100,000 and also pay money market rates. You can tap your money at any time without penalty as long as you maintain the minimum required deposit.

They are, in fact, an insured variation of the regular money market fund we just discussed in the last chapter.

The Rules and Regulations

These accounts are not very complicated, but there are a few points you should be aware of:

- Individual banks determine the minimum required.
- Penalties can be imposed if you fall below the minimum.
- You can write only three checks per month (to a third party) against your balance.
- You are allowed to withdraw money in person as often as

you like, as long as you maintain the required minimum balance.

- Usually there is no minimum amount on the size of the checks you write.

Regarding Interest Rates

The interest rate on bank money market deposit accounts is generally, but not always, just half a percentage point below that of Treasury bills. Banks adjust the rate they pay periodically, along with changes in short-term interest rates.

However, their yields tend to be a little lower than for money market funds. For example, as of 2002, the national average for bank money market deposit accounts was 3.10 percent, compared to 3.50 percent for money market funds.

A Mutual Fund or a Bank for Your Money Market?

Money Market Mutual Fund	Bank Money Market Deposit Accounts
• Best for those who switch from bonds to stocks to money market funds, as interest rates change.	• Best for those who want their savings federally insured.
• Best for those who plan to write checks against their account.	• Best for those who do not need to write more than three checks per month.
• You can write as many checks as you like, with $150 or $500 minimums per check common.	• You can write only three checks per month to third parties.
• No service charges.	• Penalties for dropping below the minimum balance.
• Not insured.	• Insured up to $100,000.

Receiving Your Interest

There is an important difference in the way in which interest is paid to depositors of bank money market deposit accounts and to shareholders in a money market mutual fund.

- Money market mutual funds must pay out most of their earnings to the fund's shareholders. Only a small percentage is retained—to cover the cost of running the fund.
- Banks, on the other hand, are not required to pay out all that your account earns. They are obliged by law, however, to post each month the interest rate they are paying.
- Although banks can pay whatever rate they want, in general you can expect bank rates to be lower than those paid on money market funds, as noted above. The reason: The money in the bank is FDIC insured. Mutual funds do not carry insurance.

Bank Money Market Deposit Account

FOR WHOM
- Investors who know they can maintain the minimum balance.
- Those who want to earn interest and have instant access to their money.
- Those seeking a safe parking place for their savings or their emergency nest egg.

MINIMUM
- Determined by individual banks; typically: $1,000, $2,000, or $2,500.

SAFETY FACTOR
- Very high.
- Insured up to $100,000.

ADVANTAGES
- Competitive interest rates.
- You can transfer money to your checking account (three preauthorized transfers per month).
- You can withdraw money in person as often as you like.
- You can take your money out easily and instantly if interest rates drop.

DISADVANTAGES
- Some banks impose penalties for withdrawal.
- You must maintain a minimum balance.
- You can write only three checks per month.
- If your balance falls below the minimum, you may lose interest or be hit with a charge.

SOME SPECIAL TIPS
- Find a bank money market deposit account that can be linked electronically to other accounts and to the bank's ATM. Then you can write more than the three minimum checks since there's no limit on how often you can personally make transfers.

  In other words, if the accounts are connected, you can keep most of your money in the higher-paying MMDA and transfer funds into your checking account only as you need to do so.
- Select a bank that allows you to connect your MMDA to a brokerage account so you can buy stocks, bonds, and Treasuries by phone.
- Look at the effective annual yield when comparing banks. It is easier to compare this figure than to try to decipher each bank's individual compounding methods.
- Find out if your interest rate will be lowered to the passbook rate if your account falls below the minimum.
- Use a bank that cuts the rate only for the days when your balance is below the minimum, not one that penalizes you for the entire week or month.

7 Certificates of Deposit

Certificates of deposit, called CDs, are time certificates sold by banks. They are issued for a specific dollar amount for a specific length of time.

If you are looking for safety and fairly competitive yields, this is the place for you. All you need to do is agree to leave a certain amount of money with the bank or credit union for the stated time period—anywhere from a few months to several years. When that time period is up, your CD "matures" or "comes due" and you get the full amount back, plus interest.

CDs purchased at FDIC-insured institutions are insured for up to $100,000. Minimum deposits vary from several hundred dollars to several thousand. Huge CDs—those of $100,000 and up—are called jumbo CDs. They pay higher rates than lower-denomination CDs.

CDs with Unique Twists

Banks offer a number of variations on the traditional CD. Ask around. You may encounter one of these or something equally appealing:

- *Bump-up CDs*. Great if interest rates are moving up. You can move to a higher interest rate, usually once, during the term of the deposit.
- *Built-in CDs*. These carry built-in rate increases.
- *Penalty-free CDs*. Rather rare, but nice. You can withdraw a portion of your money without a penalty within a certain time frame.

What a Difference a Bank Makes

Because banks have various types of CDs, it is absolutely essential that you shop around. Don't assume that all institutions have more or less the same rates because it's just not true.

The national average for six-month CDs, as of 2002, was 3.8 percent, yet CDs were available for as high as 4.7 percent.

CDs versus Other Cash Alternatives

VERSUS MONEY MARKET ACCOUNTS AND FUNDS

Although CDs of one year or less tend to pay slightly higher rates than bank money market accounts, you give up immediate, penalty-free access to your money.

VERSUS TREASURY NOTES

Before you buy a longer-term CD, compare its rate with that of a Treasury note (see Chapter 12). An advantage that T-notes offer is that their interest is free from state and local taxes. This is not true for CDs—their interest is fully taxed.

Minimums also vary. Rates vary. Compounding methods vary. Maturities vary. Penalties for cashing in early vary. Yet, in general, you will find that:

- Interest rates on similar CDs offered by different banks in the same city can vary by as much as 1 percent or more.
- You will earn more on your CD if the interest is compounded daily.
- Some banks "tier" their interest rates, which means they pay higher interest on larger deposits.
- Banks can set any maturities they wish.

CD Checklist

- Call two or three banks as well as your broker or a discount broker to see who has the highest rate.
- Ask how the interest is calculated. Remember, daily is far better than weekly or quarterly.
- Review rates. You may get a slightly higher rate from a broker because the firm buys huge certificates of $100,000 or more and then sells them to the public in $1,000, $5,000, or $10,000 chunks. You may also get a higher rate because brokerage firms shop the nation's banks, seeking the highest yielding CDs.
- Know how your interest will be handled. Have it reinvested so you won't spend it.
- Find out the rating (that is, the financial standing) of the bank issuing the CD—if you're buying it from a broker. Merrill Lynch, for example, provides credit ratings on all its CDs.

Some banks will let you set your own maturity date in what are called "designer CDs." If you have to prepare for college tuition, for instance, you can buy a CD that comes due when your child goes off to school in September. Designer CDs are also ideal for anyone expecting a baby or retiring at a certain date.

☀️ **Hint** Watch for periodical local interest-rate wars and take advantage of temporarily higher rates and favorable terms during this time period.

Buying a CD from Your Broker

In addition to being able to buy CDs at your bank, you can also buy them through a stockbroker. The advantage: You escape those hefty early-withdrawal penalties that the banks impose. Why is this? You can sell your bank CD back to the brokerage firm you purchased it from before it matures.

Note: CDs sold by brokers pay the same rates as the banks that issued them and they are FDIC insured.

How It Works

First, you tell your broker what CD maturity you want. He will quote a rate. Since the bank pays the broker to sell its CDs, you will not be stuck paying your broker a commission. Then you proceed to buy the CD.

Second, if you want to redeem your CD before maturity, you can sell it back to the broker without a penalty. Your broker can readily sell it to someone else in what is called the "secondary market."

✋ **Caution** The price of the CD will fluctuate depending upon what it's worth on the open market. In other words, your CD will go up in price if interest rates go down—that's because it is more prized by investors than newly issued CDs that are paying lower rates. That means it is possible to make a profit by actually cashing in a CD before its maturity date. On the other hand, your CD will decrease in value if money market rates rise.

Choosing a CD Interest Rate

Advertising by financial institutions may herald high rates in order to entice you and your money. But before you buy a CD from a bank, read the fine print and figure out the true interest rate. Here's what you need to look for:

- *Compounding.* Note whether the ad indicates whether interest is compounded or simple. Compounded is better because it means your interest earns interest. On a one-year CD that pays 5 percent simple, your interest rate is just that—5 percent. But when it's compounded daily, that 5 percent yields the equivalent of 5.33 percent over the course of a year.
- *Teaser Rates.* Some CDs offer a really high introductory rate, which then, of course, drops. The high rate is apt to appear in the ad in boldface, whereas the lower rate will be in the fine print. Ask how long the high rate will be in effect.
- *Rollover Rates.* Find out if you will be notified when your CD is coming due; if you are not and you forget, will it be rolled over into another CD? If so, the new CD might be paying a lower rate—something you certainly want to avoid.

☼ **Hint** Check the Wednesday edition of the *Wall Street Journal*, the Friday edition of *USA Today*, or your Sunday newspaper for a listing of the highest yielding CDs. You will find continually updated lists at: www.bankrate.com. Make certain any CD you buy is FDIC-insured.

Mini-Investor Programs

Once you have tucked away a small nest egg, believe it or not, $500 can move you into the stock market. There are several interesting programs designed for the mini-investor, but remember, stocks are much riskier than any of the previously discussed investments.

🖐 **Caution** These mini-programs are *not* designed to replace your savings. They are merely an inexpensive way to buy stocks—they sidestep using a stockbroker and/or offer reduced commissions. Please do not participate until you have saved at least three months' worth of living expenses in your money market account or in several bank CDs.

What Exactly Is a Stock?

Before becoming involved in the stock market, it's only logical that you understand what a stock is.

A stock represents part ownership in a company, and anyone who owns a stock is called a stockholder or shareholder. When a company wants to raise capital (usually to expand), it can do several things: It can borrow the money from the bank, it can issue (or sell) stocks to the public, or it can sell bonds. (Stocks and bonds are discussed in greater detail in Chapters 17 and 18.)

In order to document the fact that someone has purchased a stock, the company issues stock certificates to shareholders. This piece of paper shows the number of shares purchased at any one time by that person. If you buy more shares subsequently, you'll be given yet another stock certificate.

Making Money in Stocks

If the company is profitable, you, as a shareholder, can make money in two ways: through dividends and/or appreciation. A **dividend** is a periodic payment (almost always a cash payment) made from a company's earnings to stockholders. Most dividends are paid out four times a year. The board of directors can increase, decrease, or even cancel dividends, depending upon the company's profits.

Dividend payments vary from company to company. In fact, some never pay dividends. Those that consistently do are known as income stocks and investors buy them precisely because they want the steady cash payments. Utility stocks, discussed in Chapter 13, are known as income stocks.

The stocks of companies that pay no dividends, or very small ones, are known as **growth stocks.** Profits are reinvested in the company rather than used to make dividend payments. Investors buy them because they expect the price of the stock to grow over time. Growth stocks are riskier than income stocks, but they offer greater money-making potential; they are discussed in Chapter 18.

Buying Stocks

You may buy stocks in any publicly held corporation—one whose shares are traded publicly. (Some companies are privately held and do not sell shares to the public.) In addition to individuals, institutions also buy stocks. **Institutional investors** include mutual funds and employee pension funds.

Stocks are sold to the public in two steps: initially in the **primary market,** and thereafter these same stocks are resold to other investors through a stock exchange in what is called the **secondary market.**

The secondary market is not any one place but includes the New York, American, and regional stock exchanges as well as the over-the-counter or NASDAQ market. The exchanges are actually marketplaces where certain qualified stocks, approved by the exchange, may list their shares for buying and selling, known as trading.

Note: Although the price of a stock is fixed when it is initially offered to the public, its price thereafter continually fluctuates.

Here are ways you can get into the action with your $500.

Buying Stock Directly

A growing number of companies will let you make your first stock purchase directly from the company without a service fee. Hundreds of others offer this service for a small fee. Among those that do not charge a fee:

American Water Works
Bank One
Brunswick Corp.
El Paso Corp.
Gannett Co.
Home Depot
Huntington Bancshares
Maytag
NewsCorp, Ltd.
Schering Plough
Sherwin-Williams
Wrigley

Dividend Reinvestment Plans

It Pays to Be a DRIP

No one likes to pay brokerage commissions, even to a friendly broker. In fact, commissions prevent some small investors from buying stocks at all, which is a shame.

Here's yet another way around this dilemma: Over a thousand companies allow existing shareholders to participate in a DRIP (Dividend Reinvestment Program). Here's how they work: You must already own stock in a company. Then you can buy additional shares by automatically reinvesting your dividends.

A number of blue-chip companies, such as AT&T, Clorox, DuPont, Heinz, Texaco, Procter & Gamble, and Kellogg, that pay above-average dividends have DRIPs. Some charge a nominal fee, but none charge what a broker would.

Some also offer 3 to 5 percent off the market price of new shares for even greater savings. Many allow shareholders to make cash payments into the plan in order to accumulate more shares in their accounts. Dividend investment is done entirely through the company.

🔆 **Hint** If you already own stock in a company, call the Shareholder Relations Division and ask if it has a DRIP and, if so, how many shares you need to enroll. Or log on to the company's website. With some, a single share is sufficient; others require 50 or 100 shares.

Here are 22 DRIPS with minimum purchases of just $250:

American Electric Power	McCormick & Co.
Calgon Carbon	Office Depot
Delta Air Lines	Penney (J.C.)
Duke Energy	Peoples Energy
Exxon-Mobil	Procter & Gamble
Freddie Mac	Sunoco Products
General Electric	Southern Co.
Heinz (H.J.)	Texaco
Home Depot	Tyson Foods
Kelly Services	Wal-Mart Stores
Lowe's Companies	Wells Fargo

💡 **Hint** For a complete listing of companies with DRIPs, contact: Horizon Publishing Co.
7412 Calumet Ave
Hammond, IN 46324
800-233-5922
Horizon has an annual directory ($7.95) and a monthly newsletter called *The DRIP Investor.*

Two More Low-Cost Ways to Buy Stocks

- *Buying One Share.* Individual investors may join the National Association of Investment Clubs (NAIC). Under NAIC's Low-Cost Investment Plan, for a one-time charge of $7 per company, you can buy as little as one share of stock, directly from more than 150 major participating corporations.

    Among the companies are: Exxon-Mobil, PepsiCo, Kellogg, Volvo, and Wendy's. Although most do not charge a commission, many require a minimum investment of $25 to $250 and/or a setup fee, typically $7.

- *Buying at Work.* An increasing number of companies offer plans through which employees can buy stock in the company they work for. These are called ESOPs, or Employee Stock Ownership Plans.

Selected Stocks: One Share Minimum

A number of companies will let you sign up for their dividend reinvestment plan even if you own just one share. Ten that do:

American Water Works (AWK)	Maytag (MYG)
Bank One (ONE)	NewsCorp, Ltd. (NWS)
Brunswick Corp. (BC)	Schering Plough (SGP)
El Paso Corp. (EPG)	Sherwin-Williams (SHW)
Gannett (GCI)	Wrigley (WWY)

Dollar Cost Averaging

While no investment plan is 100 percent risk-free, dollar cost averaging, a technique offered by the Blueprint Program™, can help cushion you from stock market fluctuations.

With dollar cost averaging, you invest the same fixed dollar amount every month in the same stock—say $25, $50, or $100. That means you buy more shares when prices go down and fewer when prices go up. Over the long run, you get a lower average cost per unit for the investments you make.

Note: You can cancel this plan at any time. You can also use dollar cost averaging on your own or with mutual funds.

Check with your benefits officer to see if your employer offers this option. However, never invest all your money in your own company—even the best have their ups and downs.

The BUYandHOLD.com Program

This Wall Street–based company is specifically designed to help the small investor. At their website, www.BUYandHOLD.com, you can open a brokerage account for as little as $20. So those who felt shut out of the market in the past now have an opportunity to move from saver to investor and build a solid portfolio of growth stocks.

BUYandHOLD.com, in fact, is one of the few places where you can invest such a small amount. Even Uncle Sam's minimum for purchasing an EE Savings Bonds is $50 and mutual funds typically require $1,000 or more to get started.

Among its features:

1. Easy purchase of fractional shares of over 4,100 stocks and 49 Index Shares.

2. Electronic transfers from your bank account to purchase stocks on a weekly, monthly, or quarterly basis through their dollar cost averaging program, called E-ZVest.

3. Free reinvestment of stock dividends.

4. Special accounts for kids.

5. Affordable pricing plans, starting at just $6.99 per month, based on what you think is right for you.

6. Real-time trades for just $19.99 each.

7. Easy-to-understand online account statements.

8. Specific weekly buy, hold, and sell stock recommendations made by financial experts. (Called the BUYandHOLD Advisory Services, there is a small fee for this advice.)

The company's goal is to break the myth that "market timing" is a wise investment strategy for building personal wealth. As Peter E. Breen, CEO and cofounder of BUYandHOLD, explains, the company has "created a place where customers can feel comfortable about learning the ropes of long-term investing [because we] offer them the information needed to demystify online investing."

And, indeed, the user-friendly site is a godsend to those who feel helpless when it come to picking stocks. Experts provide daily commentary on the market and answer questions from clients on an individual basis.

BUYandHOLD.com is also home to several hundred investment clubs who share a common philosophy that long-term investing is best.

Experts point out that long-term investing also pays off in terms of taxes. If you sell stock that you've owned for more than 12 months at a profit, your gain is taxed at the lower long-term rate of 20 percent. But sell shares before a year is up and your gain is taxed at your regular rate, which could be as high as 39.6 percent.

To learn more about tucking away stock on a regular basis, click on: www.buyandhold.com.

Investment Clubs

Of all the options you have at your doorstep, a clubhouse will provide you with the most fun and enjoyment—if not the greatest return on your principal.

Joining an investment club is an excellent way to learn about the stock market, the movement of interest rates, and the overall economy. It's also a way to meet new people who, like you, are interested in learning how to turn a small amount of money into a sizable chunk.

Most clubs are small—the optimum size is about 20—and they meet once or twice a month in a community center or in a member's home. Members pool their money and jointly decide what stocks to purchase and when to sell.

Clubs require monthly payments that range from $20 per month to as high as the members dare go—several thousand dollars in some cases. Energetic hosts frequently combine the regular business meeting and discussion with coffee, dessert, or other refreshments.

How Clubs Work

The mechanics are simple. Making money, though, is not, especially if most members are inexperienced. Nevertheless, you will get your investment feet wet, and by combining your collective dollars and knowledge, you'll undoubtedly pick a winner or two, if not more!

If you don't know of a club in your area, ask at work or at your local YMCA or YWCA, adult education center, church, or synagogue.

Can't find one? Why not start your own with a few friends or colleagues? The eight steps are quite simple:

1. Find 12 to 20 people willing to join a club. Set the minimum investment requirement ahead of time—typically $30 to $100/month.

2. Select a person to be responsible for the paperwork. This task should rotate every few months.

3. Get details on how to get started from: The National Association of Investors Corp., 711 West 13 Mile Road, Madison Heights, MI 48071; 810-583-6242. Or click on: www.better-investing.org. This is the umbrella group for all clubs. Your club may join NAIC for $40, plus $14 per member. You will then receive a stack of useful literature plus a subscription to *Better Investing* magazine.

The NAIC also gives member clubs extremely useful and really solid advice on the legal aspects of organizing a club, conducting meetings, analyzing stocks, and setting up portfolios.

How Monthly Savings Add Up

Look at what happens if you invest $100, $300, or $500 each month at the fixed rate of 8 percent, not taking taxes into consideration.

Monthly Amount	5 Years	10 Years	20 Years
$100	$7,348	$18,295	$58,902
$300	$22,043	$54,884	$176,706
$500	$36,738	$91,473	$294,510

(Source: Credit Union National Association, Inc.)

Investment Clubs

FOR WHOM
- Anyone.

MINIMUM
- Set by individual clubs. Ranges from $30/month and up.
- Members contribute a set dollar amount each month.

SAFETY FACTOR
- Depends on the club's investment philosophy.

ADVANTAGES
- Inexpensive and supportive way to learn about investing.
- Reduces anxiety surrounding first-time investing and trading stocks.
- Individual members of the NAIC can buy one share of any of a number of companies and thereafter invest small amounts periodically in these companies.

DISADVANTAGES
- You may earn a better return elsewhere, especially if your club is inexperienced or does not set sensible buy-and-sell guidelines.
- Results are not guaranteed.
- Investments are not insured.
- There's a high mortality rate, with many clubs failing in the first 12 to 18 months.

  ☞ **Help!** *The Millionaire's Club: How to Start and Run Your Own Investment Club* (New York: Wiley, 2000; $19.95).

💡 **Hint** Individuals can join NAIC for just $40. You should even if you're not a member of a club.

4. Establish firm guidelines regarding withdrawal of a member's funds and entry of new members.

5. Meet and invest on a regular basis—whether the market is doing well or not.

6. Reinvest all earnings in a diversified portfolio—one that has at least five different companies.

7. Use a discount broker to save on commissions.

8. Stick to regular stock buy-and-sell guidelines. All members should be responsible on a rotating basis for doing research and making recommendations to the club.

Do Clubs Really Make Money?

Yes, a great many of them do. According to a recent NAIC survey, most clubs bettered the S&P 500's total return. And the NAIC's Index (of the stocks most widely held by member clubs) has performed well: for the five years ending December 29, the NAIC's total return was 21.5 percent versus 16.5 percent for the S&P 500 Index.

NAIC clubs adhere to these four basic principles:

- Invest regular sums of money once a month in common stock. This helps you obtain a lower average cost on your investments.
- Reinvest all earnings, dividends, and capital gains. Your money grows faster if earnings are reinvested. This way, compounding of your money is at work for you.
- Buy growth stocks—companies whose sales and earnings are increasing at a rate faster than the industry in general. They should have good prospects for continued growth, or in other words, they should be stronger, larger companies five years from now.
- Invest in different industries. Diversification helps spread both risk and opportunity.

PART THREE

THE FIRST $1,000

10 Your IRA, Keogh, or SEP

Without a doubt, the very first $1,000 that you manage to accumulate above and beyond your emergency nest egg should be invested in a tax-advantaged retirement plan: an **IRA** (Individual Retirement Account), a **Keogh Plan**, a Simplified Employee Pension Plan, also known as a **SEP**, or a **401(k)** plan at work.

In all of these, the money you invest grows free of taxes until you take it out. That means interest and dividend income accumulates on a tax-deferred basis.

We'll look at IRAs, Keoghs, and SEPs in this chapter and at 401(k)s in the next. (A 401(k) plan is one in which your company deducts a certain amount from your salary upon your request and puts it into a retirement account. It is also known as a salary-reduction plan.)

Why You Must Have a Retirement Plan

Life expectancy for an American baby born today is about 73½ years. That means most of us will probably spend about 20 years or so in retirement. It goes without saying that preparing for those years is an absolute necessity unless we want to face melted cheese and tuna casseroles for dinner day in and day out.

And don't count on Social Security or government-supported medical benefits—these programs are continually under attack and their future remains questionable. It's best to regard Social Security in particular only as a way to pay for a very small portion of your retirement needs. As it is, at most, Social Security benefits replace only 24 percent of salary for someone earning $60,000 upon retirement and 43 percent of salary for someone earning $24,090.

Companies have wised up, too, and are not always inclined to be any more generous than they have to be. Pension plans have been trending downward and benefits are generally being reduced.

All About Deductible IRAs

The most common type of retirement account and the one available to the greatest number of people is an IRA.

- Anyone who is working can put up to 100 percent of the first $3,000 he or she earns annually into a traditional IRA every year. If you earn less than $3,000 a year—let's say $2,275—you could contribute that entire amount. But even if you're a rock star making millions of dollars every year, $2,000 is still the maximum you can contribute annually.

- You can open an IRA at your bank or brokerage firm, with a mutual fund company, or with many insurance companies. The paperwork is simple and you actually have until April 15 to contribute money for the previous tax year.

- Although there is a maximum yearly contribution of $3,000, your IRA will increase in value just through the interest earned or the dividends paid out. These additional dollars stay in the account along with whatever you contribute, until you retire and begin withdrawing your money.

- If, like most retirees, you're in a lower tax bracket when you retire, there will be less of a tax bite when you do start tapping your account.

- Both husband and wife can contribute up to $3,000 each year (total $6,000) even if only one spouse earns compensation.
- If you are divorced and receive alimony, you can make an IRA contribution even if all your income is from alimony. That's because alimony is treated as earned income.
- Your contribution is tax deductible on your 1040 form, provided neither you nor your spouse is an active participant in an employer-sponsored retirement plan and you are younger than age 70½ at the end of the year.

Top Annual IRA Contributions

	2002	2003	2004	2005	2006	2007	2008+
Under age 50	$3,000	$3,000	$3,000	$4,000	$4,000	$4,000	$5,000
Age 50 plus	$3,500	$3,500	$3,500	$4,500	$5,000	$5,000	$6,000

- Even if you or your spouse is an active participant in a plan, you may still be able to deduct IRA contributions on a sliding scale; check with your accountant. The deduction is eliminated when adjusted gross income reaches $63,000 for a married couple or $43,000 for an unmarried person.
- Even if you are not eligible for the $3,000 tax deduction, you should still have an IRA. It is an easy and excellent way to accumulate tax-deferred earnings for the day when you retire.
- You may have use of your IRA dollars once a year for a 60-day period through a procedure called a rollover in which you actually take money out of one IRA account and put it into another one.

✋ **Caution** Unless your assets are in another IRA within 60 days, you will have to pay both income tax and an added 10 percent penalty tax. Some people find a rollover useful if they need cash for less than 60 days—but never take this money out unless you're absolutely certain you will put it back within the 60 days.

☞ **Help!** One of the most helpful booklets on IRAs is free. Contact your nearest Internal Revenue Service for a copy of publication #590, *Individual Retirement Arrangements (IRAs)*, or call 800-829-3676.

Advantages of a Traditional IRA

- Every dollar you contribute can be written off your tax return if you are not part of a qualified retirement plan at work or if you are single and your Adjusted Gross Income (AGI) is below $33,000 or $53,000, married. (These amounts change periodically; check with your accountant.)
- However, if you or your spouse participate in a qualified retirement plan, such as a 401(k), you still may be able to deduct some of your contribution depending upon your AGI. If you are single, head of household, or married filing separately, the full IRA deduction starts to shrink once your AGI exceeds $53,000 (married) or $33,000 (single). You cannot deduct your contribution at all if your AGI exceeds $63,000 (married filing jointly) or $43,000 (single).
- Penalties discourage IRA withdrawals prior to retirement and thus encourage saving.
- Interest, dividends, and price appreciation are tax free until withdrawn. That tax-free compounding is a powerful feature.

Disadvantages of a Traditional IRA

- IRAs are not terribly liquid. Although you can withdraw money before retirement, the penalties for doing so are stiff.

- Withdrawals made before age 59½ are subject to a 10 percent penalty with some exceptions; see the box on page 67.
- IRAs may not be used as collateral.

☞ **Tip:** Maximize your savings by putting money into your IRA as early as possible in the tax year. If you contribute at the beginning of the year instead of waiting until April 15 of the following year, your money will be earning interest for 15½ months—giving you a great head start.

The Roth IRA

This type of IRA, launched in 1998 and named after Senator William Roth, is nondeductible going in, but earnings accumulate entirely tax free. And more good news: you will not pay taxes when you start making withdrawals at age 59½ provided the account has been open for at least five years.

Like the traditional, deductible IRA, the maximum contribution is $3,000 (or $6,000 for a married couple filing jointly), less the total amount contributed to other IRAs.

The amount you can contribute to a Roth is phased out between $95,000 to $110,000 of AGI for single taxpayers and $150,000 to $160,000 for joint filers. If your AGI is above $110,000 (single) or $160,000 (married) you cannot have a Roth.

If you do qualify for a Roth IRA, you can continue contributing to it past age 70½—in fact, forever. And you are not required to take money out at age 70½ as you are with the traditional IRA. You can simply leave the money in the account and pass it on to the designated beneficiary.

☀ **Hint** The major mutual fund companies listed throughout this book have free literature to help you decide whether to have a traditional or a Roth IRA. Give any one of them a call or log on to their website.

And check out: www.financenter.com. This website has a number of financial calculators, including one for Roth conversions.

Playing Catch-up

The tax law signed by President George W. Bush in 2001 gave older workers—who haven't had the opportunity to start saving as early on in their careers as younger people—a real break. The law incorporates new catch-up contributions.

Once you reach age 50, you can make an additional IRA contribution each year. From 2002 to 2005, it is an extra $500 a year. Then, starting in 2006, the catch-up contribution will be $1,000 a year.

Traditional IRA vs. the Roth

If you qualify for a Roth, go for it. Here are four reasons why:

1. It gives you the opportunity to invest tax free for a longer time period since you don't have to withdraw money—ever.

2. You can also make contributions after age 70½ if you wish to do so.

3. And all withdrawals made after age 59½ will be tax free.

4. You can pass along a Roth IRA income-tax free to your heirs.

Converting to a Roth IRA

You can convert a Traditional IRA to a Roth if your AGI does not exceed $100,000 (married or single). Simply call the custodian of your Traditional IRA and ask what papers you need. You can even reverse the conversion without penalty up until October 15 of the year after the year in which the conversion took place.

There are, however, tax consequences of converting. The market value of the assets you move to a Roth (minus your nondeductible contributions) are considered taxable income.

-ღ- **Hint** Before you convert, run the numbers through the calculator at: www.quicken.com. (Click on "Retirement" on the home page.)

The Keogh Plan

If you are self-employed, either part-time or full-time, you should take advantage of the tax benefits offered by a Keogh Plan. Keoghs are available to self-employed individuals or partners, including sole proprietors who file Schedule C or a partnership whose members file Schedule E. A Keogh is usually better than a SEP (described below) for self-employed people with high, stable earnings.

ٜ؞ٜ **Hint** Even if you have a 401(k) or other qualified pension plan for your salaried income, you can still have a Keogh in which to shelter that portion of your income that comes from being self-employed. Don't miss this opportunity!

As with an IRA, you have a number of custodian choices: banks, brokerage firms, mutual funds, and insurance companies. You can deduct your contributions from your federal income tax and the assets in your account grow tax-deferred until withdrawn. The same early withdrawal penalties that apply to an IRA apply to a Keogh.

The great advantage the Keogh has over an IRA, including the IRA SEP (described on p. 64), is the high maximum contribution you can make. In fact, Keoghs offer self-employed workers the ability to set aside the largest amount of money in a retirement plan. (With an IRA, as you know, the current maximum is $3,000 a year or $3,500 if you are over age 50.)

There are several types of Keoghs: a Money Purchase Plan, a Profit Sharing Plan, and a Defined Benefit Plan.

With a **Money Purchase Plan,** contribution is mandatory; you must make the same percentage contribution each year, whether you have profits or not. You can contribute 25 percent of self-employed earnings, up to $35,000.

With a **Profit Sharing Plan,** the contribution can change each year. Currently you can contribute up to 13.045 percent of self-employed earnings, up to a maximum of $25,500.

With a **Defined Benefit Plan**, which is complicated to administer because an actuary must determine the deduction for contributions every year, the benefit is determined by averaging your highest earnings in three consecutive years.

Note: These dollar amounts and percentages are periodically changed.

🔆 **Hint** For a full discussion of Keoghs and to determine which plan is right for you, go to: www.401kafe.com. After reading this material, consult your accountant.

IRA SEPs

A SEP (Simplified Employee Pension) can be set up by an independent contractor or anyone who is self-employed or has a small business with 25 employees or less. In fact, you don't even have to be incorporated to qualify for a SEP. The paperwork is much easier to handle than with a Keogh.

However, the amount you can contribute is less. The most you can contribute is 25 percent of your annual salary.

The SIMPLE IRA

The Savings Incentive Match Plan for Employees was created by the Small Business Protection Act of 1996 to help those who work at small companies to save for retirement in a tax-deferred account.

A company can offer a SIMPLE plan if it has 100 employees or less, counting employees who earned at least $5,000 in salary in the past year. Employees can make pretax contributions—up to $6,500 this year and $7,000 next year. That amount goes up by $1,000 each year from 2003 to 2005, when it will be $10,000.

If a company offers a SIMPLE IRA, it must match your contribution dollar for dollar—up to 3 percent of your annual salary or make a nonelective 2 percent contribution to all employees. Your pretax contributions come out of your salary.

✋ **Caution** You will be hit with a 25 percent penalty if you withdraw money from the plan before you reach age 59½ and during the first two years you are enrolled in the plan. (In most other plans, the penalty for early withdrawal is only 10 percent.)

Where to Invest Your IRA, Keogh, or SEP

Whether you're inclined to be conservative or speculative, there's an investment program that's just right for your IRA, Keogh, or SEP. Several "custodians" are officially approved as places to set up these accounts—banks, brokerage firms, and mutual funds are the most popular. Take a look at all three before opening your account, taking into consideration how much money you have, your enthusiasm for monitoring your account, and your appetite for risk.

You should also ask what the annual fee is—it's officially known as the custodial fee and generally runs somewhere between $20 and $50.

-ϙ- **Hint** Be sure to pay the annual custodial fee with a separate check for two reasons: 1. So it won't reduce your account, and 2. If you mail it by December 31, you can deduct it on your tax return if your miscellaneous expenses exceed 2 percent of your adjusted gross income.

Too Many Custodians Is Not a Good Thing

Although you can divide your IRA contributions into as many investment choices and custodians as you like (as long as you stay within the dollar limitations), be smart and limit your accounts to one or two, three at the maximum. It's much too difficult and time consuming to keep track of more.

Ten No-Load Funds for Your IRA

- Alger Capital Appreciation
- Dreyfus Large Company Value
- Dreyfus Third Century
- Fidelity Mid-Cap Stock Fund
- Janus Equity Income
- L. Roy Papp Stock Fund
- Neuberger & Berman Partners

- T. Rowe Price International
- Strong Blue Chip 100
- Strong Growth & Income Fund

The IRS lets you fund IRAs with stocks, bonds, mutual funds, government and agency issues, CDs, foreign securities, covered options, and financial and commodity futures. It does not, however, allow investments bought on margin, insurance investments, and collectible objects, except U.S. and state gold and silver coins of one ounce or less.

Using a Bank

The safest and probably the most convenient choice for a small IRA is a bank **CD** or certificate of deposit that is insured up to $100,000. Most banks charge little or nothing to set up and maintain an IRA. Some, however, impose monthly maintenance charges. That means, as in every institutional transaction, you must read the fine print carefully. (See Chapter 7 on bank CDs.)

🖑 **Caution** There's some risk involved in buying a long-term CD—one that matures or comes due in five years. That's because if interest rates go up during that five-year period, your money is tied up, unavailable for buying the newer, higher-yielding certificates. So unless rates are high, buy a one- to two-year CD so you'll have money coming due, which you can then reinvest if rates climb.

Suggested Stocks for Your IRA

These 11 conservative stocks are suggested for long-term total return:

Abbott Laboratories	Harley-Davidson
Brooklyn Union Gas	Home Depot
Exxon-Mobil	J.P. Morgan

Kellogg   Walgreen
McCormick   Wrigley
Pfizer

These 6 stocks are suggested for their dividend yields:

Alliant Energy   Penn REIT
Duff & Phelps Utility   Southern Co.
New Plan Realty   UST Inc.

The IRA 10 Percent Penalty

You will be hit with a 10 percent tax penalty if you make withdrawals from your IRA before age 59½. But there are some exceptions. The 10 percent penalty won't apply if you tap into your account:

- To pay for deductible medical expenses (those that exceed 7.5 percent of adjusted gross income.)
- To pay health insurance premiums if you have been receiving unemployment compensation for at least 12 weeks.
- To buy a first-time principal residence for yourself, your spouse, your child, or your grandchild.
- To pay qualified higher education expenses for yourself, your spouse, your child, or your grandchild.

Using a Mutual Fund

The inner workings of mutual funds are explained in great detail in Chapters 5 and 14. But as far as the pros and cons of using one for your IRA or Keogh plan are concerned, here is what you should know.

Just about all mutual funds—which are companies that pool money together from individuals in order to buy a wide variety of stocks, bonds, and Treasuries—offer IRAs. Even though you can find a mutual fund specializing in gold, commodities, or foreign stocks, your own good judgment should steer you in more sane directions. Remember—you're saving for the day when you no longer have a steady paycheck.

🔅 **Hint** Most mutual funds reduce their opening minimums for IRAs—so a fund that requires $2,500 to open may let you buy shares for as little as $500. *Ask.*

Be sure you select mutual funds that invest only in money market funds, high quality blue-chip or growth stocks—those that are likely to appreciate in value and/or pay high dividends. Funds with top-rated bonds are also suitable for an IRA.

✋ **Caution** Never put your IRA in a tax-exempt mutual fund or a tax-exempt anything. Tax-exempts have lower returns or yields than taxable ones, and since IRAs are already sheltered from taxes, you don't need that feature.

Using a Brokerage Firm

At some point down the road, when you feel confident about picking your own stocks and bonds (or you have found an excellent broker) and you have at least $5,000 in your IRA account, you may want to open a "self-directed" IRA at a brokerage firm. You can manage the money or your broker can advise you on what stocks and bonds to put in your IRA.

When your IRA is small, this type of account is not a good idea. You simply don't have enough money with which to diversify, to spread out over several different stocks and thus protect yourself in case one of the stocks you select falls in price.

In addition, the brokerage fees are high in relation to the size of your account. If eventually, however, you do decide to run your own IRA and you feel confident about picking your own stocks and bonds, use a discount broker instead of a full-service firm—you'll save on commissions.

11 Your 401(k) Plan

*I've got all the money I'll ever need if I die by four
o'clock.*
— Henny Youngman

One relatively painless way to make certain you have money to get
you past four o'clock as well as through retirement is the 401(k)
plan. Offered by many employers to employees, this savings plan
has become increasingly popular since it was authorized by Congress in the early 1980s. Not only does it provide employees with an
automatic way to save for retirement, it both reduces and defers
taxes.

With this type of retirement plan, also known as a **salary-reduction
plan**, you contribute a certain amount of your annual salary to a special retirement account that has been set up by your employer with
an authorized institution.

The contribution is deducted from your paycheck, so you don't
even miss the money. The amount deducted is listed separately
on your W-2 form, but is not included in the amount listed for

"wages, tips, other compensation." In other words, your contributions are made with pretax dollars. This contribution reduces your reportable salary, which in turn reduces your federal income tax liability.

Many 401(k)s have an added plus: The employer also contributes, in some cases matching dollar for dollar or 50 cents for each dollar the employee pays in.

Most plans let employees decide where to invest their contributions. The typical choices are the company's stock, a stock mutual fund, a long-term bond fund, a money market fund, and a guaranteed investment contract (GIC). (GICs are fixed-income investments sponsored by insurance companies with payment of interest and return of principal guaranteed by the insurer but not by the federal government.)

Generally, you can move your money among the different investments at least once a year.

🖐 **Caution** Although taxes are postponed until you start receiving the money, there is a 10 percent penalty tax for withdrawing money before age 59½. (See page 71 for the recent change in tax law that allows for medical exceptions.) And you must start taking distributions by age 70½.

Each company has its own particular rules. Ask your benefits officer to explain yours and to give you a written copy of the plan's guidelines and options.

💡 **Hint** Even if you are eligible for a tax deduction on your IRA, contribute to a 401(k), too. Why? The ceiling on how much you can contribute to a 401(k) is considerably higher: $3,000 versus $11,000 for 2002. That will go up by $1,000 a year until 2006, when it reaches $15,000.

Withdrawing and Borrowing Money

Withdrawing Money

Under certain circumstances, you may be able to withdraw funds before age 59½, but only if you're facing a financial hardship—for example, if you need to pay funeral or medical expenses for a member of the family or, in some cases, to pay for a principal residence or avoid eviction from your home.

The regulations, however, are very stringent. To be eligible for a hardship withdrawal, you must prove that you can't meet your needs by borrowing from a bank or tapping other savings.

Borrowing Money from Your 401(k)

Most plans, but not all, let participants borrow money—up to half the amount vested but not more than $50,000. You pay interest on the loan to your own account, typically a percentage point above **prime**. (Prime is the rate banks charge their best commercial customers.) By law, 50 percent of your balance has to stay in the account as security for the loan. The loan must be repaid at least quarterly through payroll deductions and fully within five years—unless the money goes toward purchase of a principal residence.

🔆 **Hint** The interest rate is also lower than what a bank will charge you for a personal loan and, of course, your interest payments are made back into your own account and not to a bank—a real plus.

You'll pay a 10 percent penalty on the money you withdraw, plus federal, state, and local taxes on that amount. So if you withdraw $5,000 from your 401(k) before age 59½, you would owe a $500 penalty plus taxes on the entire $5,000.

However, you may not be hit with the 10 percent penalty, depending on the rules of your particular plan, in the following circumstances:

- You become totally disabled.
- You die and your beneficiary collects the money.
- You are in debt for medical expenses that exceed 7.5 percent of your AGI.
- You have a court order to give the money to your ex-spouse, a child or dependent.
- You were fired, laid off, quit, or took early retirement—in the year you turn 55, or later.

🤝 Help!

The new tax rules about retirement plans and their portability are complex and length. Four excellent sources:

- The Tax Planet (www.taxplanet.com)
- Your 401(k) (www.401kafe.com)
- The 401(k) Help Center (www.401khelpcenter.com)
- Martin Nissenbaum, Jeffrey Bolson, and Marc Myers, *Ernst & Young's Profit from the New Tax Law.* (New York: Wiley, 2001).

12
Treasuries for
Ultrasafe Income

Blessed are the young, for they shall inherit the national debt.
    —Herbert Hoover

When Hoover was our 31st president, he probably never dreamed that our national debt could reach $5 trillion. But it has, and to help finance it, the government issues Treasuries—Wall Street-ese for Treasury bills, notes, and bonds.

Regardless of your position on our country's debt, Treasuries are among the safest of all investment vehicles. You can get in on the action with only $1,000. They have four factors very much in their favor:

- They are the safest form of investment because the U.S. government guarantees to pay you back.
- They are extremely liquid and can be sold at any time.
- The interest earned is exempt from state and local taxes.
- You can buy them through the Federal Reserve without paying a fee.

What Are Treasuries?

Where do these Treasuries come from? Uncle Sam constantly borrows money, not only to finance building battleships but also to cover the federal deficit by issuing or selling short-term Treasury bills and longer-term notes and bonds to investors. (The difference among the three—bills, notes, and bonds—is the time limit or maturity. They run from a minimum of 13 weeks to a maximum of 30 years.)

- **Treasury bills** mature in a year or less. They come in 13-, 26-, and 52-week maturities and require a minimum investment of $1,000. Instead of paying interest, they are sold at a discount; that is, below face value.

Hint You can also invest through a Treasury-only money market fund, such as American Century's Fund, which has a minimum investment of $2,500. Call 800-345-2021 for a prospectus. This fund, which invests in Treasury bills and notes, provides income that is free from state and local but not federal taxes.

- **Treasury notes** mature in 2 to 10 years and require a minimum investment of $1,000.
- **Treasury bonds** mature in 10 years or more. The minimum investment is $1,000.
- **Inflation-indexed notes**. Offered for the first time in January 1997, these 10-year notes have a new twist: Both the bond's principal value and the amount of interest paid each year will increase along with the consumer price index.

Here's a hypothetical example from the *Wall Street Journal*:

- The interest rate is set at 3 percent.
- Inflation runs at 2 percent.
- Over the next 10 years, the bond's principal value will increase 2 percent annually.
- As the principal increases, so does the dollar value of the interest paid.
- With the interest set at 3 percent annually, each year the bondholder will get interest equal to 3 percent of the bond's continually growing principal value.

U.S. Treasuries

FOR WHOM
- Investors seeking absolute safety.
- Those with a minimum of $1,000.
- Those who enjoy helping Uncle Sam.

FEE
- No fee if purchased from Federal Reserve.
- Flat fee from banks and brokerage firms.

SAFETY FACTOR
- Highest possible.
- Backed by the U.S. government.

ADVANTAGES
- Principal and interest guaranteed.
- Maximum liquidity.
- No state and local tax on interest earned.

DISADVANTAGES
- Higher returns available elsewhere.

New issues of Treasuries are sold by the government at regular, publicly announced auctions. Older issues, on the other hand, are sold through stockbrokers in what is known as the "secondary market."

Bond Basics

Before we go any further, let's find out how bonds actually work. This information applies to bonds issued by the U.S. Treasury, by corporations, and by municipalities.

Simply stated, a bond (unlike a stock) is an IOU. When you purchase a bond you are, in effect, lending your money to the issuing company or government agency. Bonds come in three types:

1. Those issued by the U.S. government and its agencies.

2. Those issued by corporations.

3. Those issued by states, towns, or municipalities, known as tax-exempt or "munis."

The issuers of the bond are obligated to pay back the full purchase price at a particular time and not before. This is called the **maturity date**.

In general, bonds fall into two time-related categories: **intermediate notes**, which mature in 2 to 10 years; and **long-term bonds**, which mature or come due in 10 years or longer.

Until your bond matures, you will receive a fixed rate of interest on your money. This is called the **coupon rate** and is usually paid out twice a year. For example, on a $1,000 bond that pays 8 percent, you receive a $40 check every six months until maturity.

For trivia buffs: The term "coupon" dates from the time when all bonds actually came with a page of attached coupons. On each specified date, the owner of the bond clipped off the coupon, took it to the bank, and exchanged it for cash.

The **face value** or denomination of a bond is also known as par value and is typically $1,000. That means bonds are sold at $1,000 when first issued. After that, their price will vary, moving up and down just as stocks do.

Depending upon the prevailing market conditions, bonds sell at **either above par** (that is, above $1,000), which is also called **at premium**; or they sell **below par** (that is, less than $1,000), which is called at a **discount**.

And just to make it all a bit more confusing, although bonds are issued and sold in $1,000 units, their prices in the newspaper are quoted on the basis of $100, not $1,000. So you must always add a zero to the published price. For example, a bond quoted at $105 is actually selling for $1,050.

The Secondary Market

After bonds have been issued, they rise and fall in price depending upon supply and demand and upon interest rates. If rates have gone up and new bonds are paying more interest, then older bonds drop in price. On the other hand, if new bonds are paying less interest, then older bonds rise in price—they are seen as being more desirable.

You can sell your bond before its maturity date in the secondary market through a stockbroker—but bear in mind that it's possible you will not get back what you paid for it, particularly if rates have gone up.

Buying Treasuries

Treasuries are first sold through auctions held periodically by the U.S. Treasury. The auctions are held primarily for major bank and government bond dealers. These large buyers determine the final interest rate; in other words, no one knows what rate a Treasury will pay until the end of the auction.

Using a Broker

Most people find it simplest to buy Treasuries through a broker. Compare your broker's rates with those of Charles Schwab and Fidelity.

- Charles Schwab charges $49 for bonds. If you purchase them via their website (www.schwab.com) you get a 20 percent discount on the fee. If you use Schwab's TeleBroker (800-626-4600), there's a 10 percent discount. To find a Schwab office near you, call: 877-476-2370.
- Fidelity charges $50 per transaction. Details are explained at: www.fidelity.com.

Using the Treasury Direct System

However, you can sidestep broker's fees by purchasing your Treasuries directly from the government in the Treasury Direct System. Late in 1998, the government got up to speed and set up this electronic system.

- To purchase Treasuries via phone, call: 800-722-2678.
- To purchase Treasuries via the Internet, go to: www.treasurydirect.gov.

PART FOUR

THE FIRST $2,000

13

Utilities and Hometown Companies

What Is a Stock?

A stock, as you recall from Chapter 8, represents part ownership in a company, and anyone who owns a stock is called a stockholder or shareholder.

Public Utility Companies

Stocks of public utility companies have traditionally been sound, high-yielding investments and as such are considered safe enough for "widows and orphans." Because of their generally solid dividends and high safety ranking, you can invest at the $1,000 level, even though other individual common stocks are better purchased with investments of $5,000 or more, or through a mutual fund.

🖐 **Caution** In general, of course, the greater the risk element in an investment, the more money you should have to cushion any losses.

Utilities are also appealing because of their dividend reinvestment plans (see Chapter 13). Some utilities even offer a discount when their shares are bought through these plans.

You should be aware, however, that the utility industry is being deregulated and is therefore increasingly competitive. That means you should invest only in utilities with strong balance sheets and the capacity to expand, either domestically or internationally—or both.

Hometown Stocks

Other stocks that beginners are often successful at picking out for their portfolios are those of local companies. If you work for a corporation whose stock is publicly traded, you're apt to be very much in the know about its financial condition, its management, its product or service, and its future.

The same is true for companies headquartered in your area. Folks who lived near Ben & Jerry's, Boston Chicken, the Pep Boys, or Snapple, or who tasted Mrs. Field's cookies, all knew about these first-rate, popular products long before the general public.

If it plays in Peoria, it's likely to play on Wall Street.

Six High-Yielding Utility Stocks

Alliant Energy	6.9%
CMS Energy Corp.	6.4
Hawaiian Electric	6.4
NorthWestern Corp.	6.4
Ameren Corp.	6.1
Empire District Electric	6.1
(Source: *Value Line*)	

How to Find Bright Lights and Hometown Talent

Begin in your own backyard:

STEP 1. Read your local paper to keep up-to-date on company news and developments.

STEP 2. Visit the local company's headquarters; ask to take a tour or meet with an official; explain that you're seriously considering buying stock.

STEP 3. Get a copy of the annual and quarterly report. You can do this in person, or in the case of your utility, by phone. Call the investor or public relations department.

Then, read through it in order to determine if:

- Earnings per share are rising.
- Dividends are increasing.
- Plant construction is completed.
- The area's population is growing.
- The company is facing any lawsuits.
- It is facing deregulation.
- It has plans to handle increased competition.

STEP 4. Track the company's stock price for several weeks by looking in the newspaper; be alert to trends up or down. Avoid buying shares at their 52-week high. (See pages 127–128 for how to read stock market tables.)

STEP 5. Call a local stockbroker for an investment opinion and research report. You can do this whether or not you have an account.

STEP 6. Compare the brokerage firm's report with that in *Value Line Investment Survey* or Standard & Poor's *Stock Reports*. These two key reference tools are available at most public libraries and brokerage offices.

Value Line ranks stocks for safety; stick with those with a #1 or #2 ranking.

STEP 7. Read any press coverage of the company's prospects or problems.

STEP 8. If you decide to buy shares, do so through a discount broker to save on commissions and sign up for the company's dividend reinvestment plan (DRIP) if it has one.

14 Stocks and Ginnie Mae Mutual Funds

Money won't buy happiness, but it will pay the salaries
of a large research staff to study the problem.
—Billy Vaughan

Vaughan probably didn't have mutual funds in mind when he made his famous statement, but he might well have. A mutual fund is a company that has a lot of portfolio managers that make investments for others—for individuals and for institutions.

When you buy into a mutual fund you are actually purchasing shares of an investment trust or corporation. Your dollars are pooled with those of hundreds of other investors, and these combined moneys are then invested and managed by a staff of professionals, known as portfolio managers.

Fund portfolios are widely diversified—among stocks of different companies, bonds of different issuers, money market papers, and Treasuries of different maturities. All this diversification helps insulate you against wide fluctuations in the prices of individual stocks.

How Mutual Funds Work

Mutual funds are **open-ended**—that is, like stocks, shares are continually available and they can be bought or sold at any time.

The price of a fund's share is called its **net asset value**, and this price or NAV is determined at the end of each business day when the fund adds up the value of the securities held in its portfolio, subtracts expenses, and divides the total by the number of shares outstanding.

How You Make Money

Mutual funds make money for shareholders in three ways:

1. They pay shareholders dividends and interest earned from the stocks, bonds, Treasuries, and money market papers held in the portfolio.

2. They pay shareholders capital gains distributions—if a stock or bond is sold at a profit.

3. Their net asset value (or share price) may rise in value if the value of the securities held in the fund increases. When this happens, your shares are worth more, and you'll make a profit should you decide to sell.

💡 **Hint** You can have your earnings—dividends and capital gains distributions—either reinvested in additional shares of the fund or have the fund send you a check.

Picking a Mutual Fund

Before beginning your search for the right fund, you need to know the difference between load and no-load funds.

Load funds, sold by stockbrokers and mutual fund salespeople, are "loaded" with a sales charge or fee. Commissions for the purchase or sale of a fund typically range from about 4 percent to 8½ percent of the total price.

Keep in mind that this means the value of the fund must escalate by that amount *before* you can break even.

💡 **Hint** Since studies show there is no overwhelming evidence that load funds outperform no-loads, you might as well find one without a load or commission and save the difference. However, some people like to buy load funds because they trust their broker's recommendations.

No-load funds have no sales commissions. You purchase shares directly from the fund itself, not through a stockbroker. You simply call the fund's toll-free number for the appropriate papers.

It is true, however, that some no-load funds have hidden fees (see box on page 87).

And now some basic advice about selecting a fund.

Step #1

Clarify your goals. You need to figure out if you want a fund for income or for growth (also known as "appreciation"). Do you want a fund that consists primarily of stocks or bonds or some of each? Do you want a high-risk speculative fund or a more conservative one?

Each fund has a different investment objective, so it is essential that you understand these differences long before buying shares.

You'll find the fund's objectives spelled out at the beginning of the **prospectus**, which is the official description of the fund, required by the Securities and Exchange Commission to be given to potential shareholders. For example, a prospectus might read: "Our primary objective is safety of principal and long-term growth through the purchase of high-quality stocks in growth areas of the economy."

Caution: Even no-load funds can charge 12b-1 fees—up to 0.75 percent of a fund's average net assets per year. An additional 0.25 percent service fee may be paid to brokers in return for providing ongoing information to shareholders. Unlike other fund fees, this one continues on and on, for every year you own shares.

Step #2

Study the types of funds. Funds fall into several broad categories. Some emphasize growth—that is, price appreciation—while others focus on income. Some provide tax-free returns; many are conservative, while others are highly speculative.

In picking a fund, be realistic about how much time you really will spend monitoring its performance. The more speculative its portfolio, the more you need to keep your eye on it in order to know when to buy more shares, or when to sell and get out.

Mutual Fund Loads or Fees

Many mutual funds have no loads (fees), some have low loads or fees, and others have outrageously high ones. Here are the key terms you need to know before investing in any mutual fund.

- **Front-End Load**. A sales commission charged when you purchase shares in a fund. These sales fees may be as high as 8.5 percent, but most are 4 to 5 percent. The load compensates brokers or salespeople who sell the funds. So if you put $1,000 in a fund with a 5 percent load, only $950 goes to work for you in the fund; the rest goes to the broker or salesperson.
- **Back-End Load**. A fee imposed when you sell your shares. A typical back-end load fund charges 6 percent if you redeem shares the first year, 5 percent the second, and so on until the charge disappears completely. If you're forced to sell your shares before the load disappears, it can be an expensive experience.
- **Redemption Fee**. Not to be confused with a back-end load, this fee is charged by some fund companies in order to discourage frequent trading. Generally, it's charged to those who sell within a year of investing in the fund.
- **12b-1 Fee**. Named after the section of law that authorized it, this fee forces shareholders to pay some of the fund's sales and advertising expenses. It can be as high as 1.25 percent of assets, or $1.25 for every $100 you invest.

The basic types of funds:

- *Aggressive or speculative funds.* These seek maximum profit, but at a fast rate, often achieved by taking greater risks than other types of funds by selling short or even by borrowing money for additional leverage. Also known as "maximum capital gains funds."

- *Industry or sector funds.* These specialize in one type of stock, such as energy or health care stocks, realty or public utilities, technology, etc.

- *Income funds.* These invest primarily in corporate bonds and are not concerned with growth or capital appreciation. Some invest in high-dividend stocks.

- *Balanced funds.* These maintain portfolios that combine common and preferred stocks and bonds. Their aim is to conserve the investor's principal, to pay current income, and to have long-term growth. Their portfolios often consist of leading companies that pay high dividends.

- *Growth and income funds.* These invest in common stock of companies that have had increasing share value and a solid record of paying dividends.

- *Municipal bond funds.* These are designed for tax-exempt income. For more on bond income funds, see page 92.

- *U.S. government income funds.* These invest in a variety of government securities: U.S. Treasury bonds, federally guaranteed mortgage-backed securities, and other government notes.

- *Index funds.* These contain a representative basket of stocks mirroring the index, such as the Standard & Poor's 500. They keep pace with the market.

- *Money market funds.* (**See** Chapter 5.)

Step #3

Study their performance record. Rating services will tell you whether a fund is making or losing money over various time periods. Many financial magazines and newspapers publish these results on a regular basis. Check for them in:

Barron's
Kiplinger's Personal Finance Magazine
Money
USA Today
Wall Street Journal

Once you've identified a type of fund, or a specific fund, read its current analysis in *Morningstar Mutual Funds*. This research service covers 1,700 mutual funds and rates them on the basis of total return, volatility, and performance. It also gives some interesting insights about the fund's portfolio manager. Updated biweekly, you can read it at your library, broker's office, or subscribe:

Morningstar

$425 a year; 3-month trial: $55

800-735-0700 or www.morningstar.com

‑ᗺ̣- **Hint** Take advantage of all of the fund's toll-free numbers. They're not there just to make transferring from one fund to another or buying and selling shares easy. Trained service reps will answer your questions about a fund's portfolio holdings, its risk factor, its objectives, its current share price, yield, and total return figures for one, five, or more years.

When to Buy or Sell Fund Shares

Even after you've selected a fund, you may be nervous about how it will react to sudden changes in the economy, to interest rates, or to the stock market. One way to resolve this problem is to keep your money in a family of funds that offers more than one type of fund under the same corporate roof. Some of the well-known fund families are: T. Rowe Price, Vanguard, Strong, Fidelity, Dreyfus, Oppenheimer.

Most funds offer free switching from one fund to another—or if there's a charge, it's a nominal one. The fund prospectus or the service rep at the 800 number will tell you if you are limited to a certain number of switches per year.

How do you know when to switch? It requires time and study, but in general:

- When interest rates fall, keep your money in a stock fund.
- When interest rates rise, switch to a money market fund or a Treasury fund.
- When the price of the stocks in a fund starts to slide, switch some of your investment into a money market fund; park your money there until you have a sense of where the economy is headed.
- When the economy is growing, switch to a stock growth fund.
- When you move up into a higher tax bracket, move into a tax-free municipal bond fund.

🔆 **Hint** No one fund should be regarded as economically viable for all times. The market is cyclical, the economy is constantly changing, and tax rulings are periodically revised—so never make an investment and think that's it. You must track the performance of all investments, including mutual funds, on a regular basis.

✋ **Caution** Many banks now sell mutual funds. But you should realize that these funds are *not* federally insured. If you wish to purchase shares in one, you must go through the same research steps as you would for any fund: Find out its investment goals, its risk factor, and, most important, its performance record.

Insomniac Trading

If you're up all night, you don't have to wait until 9 A.M. to buy or sell mutual fund shares. Discount broker T. D. Waterhouse is available 24 hours a day, seven days a week. The company charges $27 for some no-load funds, nothing for others. Ask. **INFO:** 800-233-3411.

Stock Mutual Funds

Buying shares in a stock fund is a good alternative to trying to pick from among the thousands of publicly traded individual stocks. For the small investor, the new investor, and the very busy investor, mutual funds offer diversity, professional management, liquidity, relatively low cost, and income and/or price appreciation.

You should have at least $2,000 before participating in a stock fund, because there is a greater degree of risk here than in money market mutual funds, CDs, and savings bonds. Keep in mind that if the stock market falls, so will the value of a stock fund. On the other hand, if the market is bullish, stock funds will perform well. See the box for some suggestions.

Six Growth Funds

These tend to outperform most other types of stock funds over the long term. They are best for those willing to assume a moderate degree of risk and those who can hold their shares at least two years, preferably longer.

- Strong Growth Fund
  www.strongfunds.com and 800-368-1030

- Columbia Growth
  www.columbiafunds.com and 800-547-1707

- Franklin Growth
  www.franklintempleton.com and 800-342-5236

- Guardian Park Avenue
  www.glic.com and 800-221-3253

- Lindner Fund
  www.lindnerfunds.com and 800-995-7777

- Stein Roe Young Investor
  www.steinroe.com and 800-338-2550

Ginnie Mae Funds

These funds aim for high income and minimum risk and, more often than not, succeed. Ginnie Maes, short for Government National Mortgage Association (GNMA), are actually pools of mortgages backed by the Federal Housing Administration (FHA) or the Veterans Administration (VA). They are the only securities—except for those issued by the U.S. Treasury—whose principal and interest are backed by the "full faith and credit of the U.S. government."

Six Low Risk Income Funds

- American Century Inflation-Adjusted Treasury Bond Fund
  800-345-2021 and www.americancentury.com

- Harbor Bond Fund
  800-422-1050 and www.harborfund.com

- Neuberger & Berman Limited Maturity Bond Fund
  800-877-9700 and www.nb.com

- Stratton Monthly Dividend Fund
  800-634-5726 and sss.strattonmgt.com

- Strong Short-Term Bond Fund
  800-368-1030 and www.strong.com

- Vanguard Intermediate Term U.S. Treasury Portfolio
  800-662-7447 and www.vanguard.com

🖐 **Caution** This government guarantee protects you from one thing only: default by home owners. In other words, it guarantees that interest and principal will be paid—but it does not guarantee the value of your fund shares or the interest rate.

That means your fund shares will fluctuate in price, for, like bond funds, when interest rates rise, the value of Ginnie Mae mutual funds falls, and vice versa. That's why you should buy Ginnie Mae mutual funds only if you can hold your shares long term, thus smoothing out the fluctuations in interest rates.

🔅 **Hint** You can buy a Ginnie Mae certificate for $25,000 through a broker and avoid this problem of fluctuating mutual fund share prices.

How Ginnie Mae Certificates Work

A Ginnie Mae begins when a home buyer receives a mortgage insured by the FHA or VA. The lender then combines this mortgage with many others into a pool worth at least $1 million. This certificate—a mortgage-backed security—is then sold to a broker, who in turn sells pieces of it, also known as certificates, to individuals and to mutual funds. The "pieces" are typically sold in $25,000 units.

As home owners make monthly mortgage payments, owners of certificates receive a share of the principal and interest payments on a monthly basis.

Although these are suitable for investors seeking a steady stream of income, *they have one problem*: When interest rates fall, home owners rush to pay off their mortgages ahead of schedule and refinance at lower rates. When that happens, investors who own Ginnie Mae certificates receive their principal and interest payments sooner than planned. These investors then face the problem of reinvesting this money at the then prevailing rate, which of course is lower than when they purchased their certificates.

How Ginnie Mae Funds Work

A fund operates quite differently from the certificates. You purchase shares of one of the funds. The fund manager buys and sells Ginnie Mae certificates in much the same way a bond fund manager trades bonds.

Therefore, with a fund, *your yield is not fixed*. The yield will rise and fall in relation to interest rates. And, of course, the fund's success also depends on the ability of the manager to buy and sell certificates at the most optimum time.

Ginnie Maes

FOR WHOM
- Investors who want a high yield.

WHERE TO PURCHASE
- Directly from a fund or through stockbrokers.

FEE
- Load funds charge a sales fee (3 percent to 8.5 percent).
- No-load funds do not impose fees.

SAFETY
- Relatively high, especially if held long term.

MINIMUM
- $1,000 for funds; $25,000 for certificates.

ADVANTAGES
- Yields tend to be slightly higher than Treasuries.
- Provides monthly income.
- You can reinvest income in additional fund shares.

DISADVANTAGES
- Fund yields are not guaranteed and could drop.
- Some funds are allowed to sell options against their portfolios to keep the yields high; this adds to the risk level.
- The price or net asset value of a fund's shares can drop.

💡 **Hint** Most major no-load (no-fee) mutual funds offer Ginnie Mae funds.

🤝 **Help!** Many no-load fund families have a wealth of information on their websites—not only about their particular funds, but also about the Roth IRA, the Education IRA, saving for college, retirement planning, and asset allocation.

My six picks, in alphabetical order:

www.federatedinvestors.com

www.fidelity.com

www.monetta.com

www.strong-funds.com

www.troweprice.com

www.vanguard.com

The Investment Company Institute's pamphlet "A Guide to Mutual Funds" is available for 35 cents. Call: 202-326-5800 or click on: www.ici.org

These two letters advise readers on how and when to move among the various mutual funds. Ask for a sample copy before subscribing.

- *Fabian Investment Resource* ($119/year; monthly)
  7811 Montrose Road
  Potomac, MD 20854
- *The No-Load Fund Investor* ($139/year; monthly)
  410 Sawhill River Rd.
  Ardsley, NY 10502
  800-252-2042 and www.sheldonjacobs.com

15 Socially Conscious Mutual Funds

Is it possible to be a successful investor and socially responsible at the same time?

Yes. "Socially conscious" or "green" funds are set up so investors can reconcile their desire for profits with their concern about environmental, political, and social issues. Unlike most mutual funds, which base their portfolios primarily on financial considerations, these funds apply other criteria, called "social screens," to the selection process.

Although each fund's screen differs, most refuse to invest in weapons manufacturers and utilities that rely on nuclear power. Some screen out the so-called sin stocks: tobacco, liquor, and gambling, as well as companies that are heavy polluters. Many avoid companies that use animals for testing or that lack a strong policy of hiring and promoting women, gays, and minorities.

Here are some picks in various categories:

Growth Stock Funds

These invest in stocks expected to provide long-term capital appreciation for shareholders. They have more volatile price swings than the more conservative income and balanced funds, described next.

- Calvert Equity: 800-368-2748 and www.calvert.com
- Dreyfus Premier Third World Century: 800-645-6561 and www.dreyfus.com
- Pioneer Capital Mid-Value: 800-225-6292 and www.pioneer-funds.com
- Parnassus Fund: 800-999-3505 and www.parnassus.com

Income Funds

- Calvert Social Investment Bond: 800-368-2748
- Pioneer Bond Fund: 800-225-6292
- Citizens Income Fund: 800-1223-7020

Balanced Funds

These funds seek the highest possible return consistent with a low-risk strategy. Their portfolios contain both stocks and bonds. They typically have higher dividend yields than growth funds and perform better when stocks are falling in price. In a rising market, however, they do not keep pace with growth funds.

- Pax World Balanced Fund: 800-767-1729
- Calvert Social Investment Balanced Portfolio: 800-368-2748

Money Market Funds

These funds do not invest in U.S. Treasury issues because, they maintain, those issues are used primarily to finance a federal deficit largely caused by heavy defense spending. Instead, these funds purchase issues of the Federal Farm Credit System, the Small Business Administration, and other government agencies.

- Citizens Trust: 800-533-3863
- Calvert Money Fund: 800-368-2748
- Domini: 800-762-6814

Index Funds

These three funds follow an index made up of stocks of socially responsible companies:

- Calvert Social Index Fund
- Citizens Core Growth Fund
- Domini Social Equity Fund

☞ **Help!** For more information:

Socially Responsible Funds (www.socialfunds.com) A comprehensive website on socially responsible investing, with coverage of social mutual funds, community investment, and shareowner action.

Social Investment Forum (www.socialinvest.org) This site is devoted to socially responsible investing, with a list of financial professionals knowledgeable about socially responsible investing.

16 Index Funds

A No-brainer

These fund are designed to keep pace with the market or a certain segment of the stock market. That's all they do. Don't expect more. Don't expect less.

But for an investor who does not want to keep close track of the market, an index fund can be a good solution.

It's critical, however, that you understand an index fund's returns will parallel the market—up in a good market, down in a poor market. It is very much a form of passive investing—in fact, much of it is done by computer—and you don't belong in an index fund if you think you'll cave in and bail out after one quarter or one year of poor performance.

An index fund consists of a basket of stocks that mimic a particular index, and therefore its performance mirrors that of the index, such as the S&P 500, the Small Cap Index, or the Lehman Brothers Bond Market Index. There are also index funds for REITs (Real Estate Investment Trusts), international stocks, and socially responsible investing.

Advantages

1. **A no-brainer.** Index funds offer an easy way for you to participate in the long-term growth of a particular segment of the market, or the entire market, at a relatively low cost.

2. **Inexpensive.** Index funds are inexpensive for mutual funds to operate. They don't need to pay a hotshot portfolio manager to decide what stocks or bonds to buy and when to sell them. And they don't require large research staffs. These funds sell shares only when a stock is deleted from an index or when net redemptions force stock sales. The average stock fund has an expense ratio of about 1.4 percent versus a little under 1 percent for an index fund. That means more of your money is invested.

3. **Low taxes.** Taxes are not a major factor. These funds rarely sell their shares, so their capital gains distributions are far less than for actively managed funds. Therefore, you're unlikely to be hit with a capital gains tax until you sell your shares. Fewer taxable distributions make these funds a real plus for money invested outside retirement accounts.

4. **Diversification**. These funds provide excellent diversification.

5. **No surprises.** You know precisely what stocks you're invested in at all times.

6. **No underperformance.** You will not underperform the market.

7. **No management changes.** You don't have to worry about a portfolio manager leaving the fund.

Sheldon Jacobs, editor of the monthly *No-Load Fund Investor*, recommends dividing your money as follows, provided you are only invested in index funds and you have a long-term horizon:

- Vanguard Total Stock Market Index: 50 percent
- Vanguard Small Cap Stock Fund: 20 percent
- Vanguard International Equity Index: 10 percent
- Vanguard Short-Term Bond: 10 percent
- Vanguard Intermediate Term Bond: 10 percent

The Total Stock Market Index replicates the entire U.S. stock market. The Small Cap follows the Russell 2000 index of small-cap stocks. The International Equity Index is split evenly between the European index and the Pacific index.

💡 **Hint** If you're investing a lump sum, do so gradually. This lessens the risk of buying at the market peak. Many mutual fund companies will move money once a month or once a quarter from their money market fund into stock or bond mutual funds.

The Major Indexes

Index funds are largely based on the well-known traditional indexes, although there are also some obscure indexes. Here's a thumbnail sketch of the most important indexes.

- **Dow Jones Industrial Average (DJIA).** A price-weighted average of 30 blue-chip stocks, representing the overall price movement of all stocks traded on the New York Stock Exchange. It is determined by adding up the closing prices of the component stocks and using a divisor that is adjusted for splits and stock dividends.

- **Standard & Poor's Composite Index of 500 stocks (S&P 500).** Unlike the Dow, the S&P 500 is market-weighted. That is, its component stocks are weighted according to the market value of their outstanding shares. The result: the impact of any single component's price change is proportional to its overall market value.

- **Standard & Poor's 400 Midcap Index.** Comprised of 400 domestic companies. The median market capitalization of stocks in this index is $610 million versus about $2.2 billion for stocks in the S&P 500.

- **Wilshire Equity 5000 Index.** Covers the entire U.S. stock market. However, it is still dominated by the large caps. The largest 500 stocks represent about 82 percent of the index's total value. This means the Wilshire usually tracks the S&P 500, with the Wilshire typically outperforming the S&P 500 in years when small stocks are the winners.

- **Nasdaq-Composite Index.** This index, which takes its name from the National Association of Securities Dealers' Automated

Quotation system, covers most of the stocks on the Nasdaq. It includes about 4,800 stocks, many of which are in the technology industry.

- **New York Composite Index.** A market-value weighted index covering the price movements of all common stocks listed on the Big Board.
- **Russell 2000 Index.** Measures the performance of the small cap stocks—the performance of the 2,000 smallest companies in the Russell 3000 Index.
- **The Russell 3000 Index.** Measures the performance of the 3,000 largest U.S. companies based on total market capitalization—about 98 percent of the U.S. equity market.
- **The Russell 1000 Index.** Measures the performance of the 1,000 largest companies in the Russell 3000 Index.
- **Value Line Composite Index.** An equally weighted index of 1,700 New York Stock Exchange, American Stock Exchange, and OTC stocks tracked by the Value Line Investment Survey.

A Directory of Index Funds

Here are a handful of funds to consider:

S&P 500 Index Funds

Dreyfus S&P 500 Index
E-Trade S&P 500 Index
Fidelity Spartan 500 Index
Schwab S&P 500 Index
Strong Index Fund
USSA S&P 500 Index
Vanguard 500 Index

Wilshire 5000 Funds

Fidelity Spartan Total Market Index
Schwab Total Stock Market Index
Vanguard Total Stock Market Index

Mid-Cap Indexes

Dreyfus MidCap Index
E-Trade Extended Market Index
Federated Mid-Cap
Vanguard Mid-Cap Index

Small-Cap Indexes

Dreyfus Small-Cap Stock Index
Federated Mini-Cap Index
Vanguard Small-Cap Growth Index
Vanguard Small-Cap Value Index

International Indexes

Dreyfus International Stock Index
Fidelity Spartan International Index
Schwab International Index
Vanguard Emerging Market Index
Vanguard Europe Index
Vanguard Pacific Index
Vanguard Total International Index

Specialized Index Funds

AON REIT Index
Citizens (Socially Responsible) Index Portfolio
Domini Social Equity Fund
Vanguard REIT Index Fund

Bond Index Funds

Dreyfus Bond Market Index
E-Trade Bond Index
Schwab Short-term Bond Market Index
Vanguard Intermediate Bond Index
Vanguard Long-term Bond Index
Vanguard Short-term Index
Vanguard Total Bond Market Index

✌ Help!

- Before investing in any particular fund, read the current evaluation of the fund in **Morningstar** (www.morningstar.com).
- For an excellent tutorial on index funds, log on to: www.indexfunds.com.
- The **Vanguard Group,** headquartered in Valley Forge, PA, has the largest number and the lowest cost index funds. Details: 800-662-7447 and www.vanguard.com.

Websites for the Indexes

- **Dow Jones Averages:** www.djindexes.com
- **Nasdaq Stock Market:** www.nasdaq.com
- **Russell Indexes:** www.russell.com
- **Standard & Poor's Indexes:** www.spglobal.com
- **Wilshire 5000:** www.wilshire.com

PART FIVE

WHEN YOU HAVE $5,000

17

Bonds: Corporates, Munis, and Zeros

"Gentlemen prefer bonds," noted Andrew Mellon. And so should women and children.

In Chapter 12 we discussed U.S. Treasury notes and bonds as the ultimate safe choice if you want steady income. There are two other types of bonds that also offer income: **corporate bonds** and **municipals.**

Corporates pay slightly higher rates than Treasuries, but they're also higher in risk. On the other hand, municipal bonds, whose yields are lower, have a great tax advantage: Their interest is exempt from income tax at the federal level and, in many cases, at the state and local levels as well.

Both corporate and municipal bonds pay a set rate of interest twice a year for the life of the bond, and if you hold the bonds until maturity, you'll get back the face value—$1,000 per bond.

Most brokerage firms require a minimum of at least $5,000 or $10,000 to buy bonds. With your $5,000 you will be able to purchase five bonds, which is not sufficient diversification to protect you against default and calls. At the $5,000 level, it's wiser to purchase a unit investment trust or bond fund; both are explained below.

However, in preparation for the day when you have $10,000 or more, let's take a look at how to find high quality bonds.

How to Select Bonds

Using Credit Ratings

Before purchasing a corporate or a municipal bond, take a minute or two to find out about the issuer's credit worthiness as reported by either Standard & Poor's or Moody's—the two leading independent rating services.

Both services periodically update their rating and publish them in huge volumes available at most public libraries and brokers' offices.

Bond Ratings

Moody's		S&P's
Aaa	Top quality	AAA
Aa	Excellent	AA
A	Very high	A
Baa	Medium	BBB
Ba	Speculative	BB
B	Lower speculative	B
Caa	Poor and risky	CCC
Ca	Near default	CC
C	In default	C

The highest rating a bond can receive is triple A. Medium-grade bonds fall into the triple B category, while those that are C or lower are speculative. In general, inexperienced and conservative investors should stick with bonds rated A or better.

A bond's yield also reflects the issuer's credit quality. Lower quality bonds, also known as noninvestment grade—those rated BB or below—generally have higher yields than better quality, safer issues. The higher yield compensates the investor for lending money to a company that is considered somewhat likely to default on its interest or principal payments.

In addition to the credit risk or financial shape of the corporation or municipality, there are two additional risk factors to bear in mind when investing in bonds: interest rate risk and the call factor, or recall risk.

- **Interest rate risk** is a problem only if you sell your bonds prior to maturity. If interest rates have climbed since your purchase, your bond may very well be worth less than when you bought it. That's because newly issued bonds, paying the new higher rates, are more prized. Of course, the opposite is also true: If rates fall, your bond will be worth more because it is still paying the old higher rate. Solution: Hold bonds until maturity.

- **Recall risk.** Believe it or not, your bonds may actually be "called in," which means they'll be taken away from you prior to maturity. This is something many investors are unaware of. Not all bonds can be called, but those that can have what is known as a "call feature." This gives the issuer the right to redeem the bond before maturity.

You receive the full face value of the bond, but you then face the problem of investing that money at the prevailing rate, which is usually lower than the one you were receiving.

How to Know if a Bond Will Be Called

The conditions for calling in a bond are provided in the statement filed with the SEC when the bonds are first issued to the public. Call features are also listed in the bond guides.

The call feature is usually not exercised if the current interest rate is the same as or higher than the bond coupon rate. But if interest rates fall below the bond's coupon rate, the bond may be called because the issuer can now borrow money at a lower rate. The issuer, in fact, may decide to take advantage of the lower rates and issue a new series of bonds. (Remember, a bond is just a loan you make to the issuer, who would naturally prefer to pay the lowest interest rate possible.)

Protecting Yourself

If a bond is called in, you then lose that steady stream of income you thought you had locked in for a given number of years. But there is a way to protect yourself from calls, which is essential when investing long term. You can buy a bond with "call protection." This guarantees that the bond will not be called for a specific number of years. Corporate bonds are likely to offer ten-year call protection. Most government bonds are not callable at all, but check carefully—contrary to popular belief, some are.

-♡- **Hint** Check with your broker to find out if a bond has call protection.

Corporate Bonds

Thousands of U.S. corporations raise money by selling bonds to the public. Some of these companies are small and obscure; others are well known. In general, it is best to stick to the bonds of leading companies and those that are traded on the New York Stock Exchange. Then if you need to sell, you can do so more easily than if you owned thinly traded bonds.

Bond prices are listed in the financial pages of the newspaper. They are quoted with fractions listed in eighths. For example, a bond listed at $98¼ sells for $982.50.

Here's what a typical listing looks like:

Name	Coupon & Maturity	Current Yield	Sales in $1,000	High	Low	Last	Change
duPont	6½ 06	6.97	39	93⅜	92¾	93¼	+⅛

The first column indicates that this E.I. duPont Corporation bond has a coupon rate of 6.5 percent and a maturity date of 2006. In other words, it pays $65 per year for every $1,000 bond, and it will do so until the year 2006.

If you divide the coupon rate (6.5 percent) by the current market price (listed under "Last" and in this example 93¼), you will get the current yield (6.97 percent).

The number of bonds traded was 39. The high was $933.75 and the low $927.50. The closing price was $932.50, up $12.50 per bond.

You may wonder why the yield for the bond rose from 6.5 percent to a current yield of 6.97 percent. The reason is that the price of the bond has gone down from $1,000 (on the first day issued) to $932.50.

Should You Buy Corporate Bonds?

Yes—if you stick with top-rated, financially solid corporations such as IBM, duPont, Eastman Kodak, Bristol Myers Squibb, and the sounder public utility companies. You will achieve a steady flow of income for the life of the bond.

Another advantage that corporate bonds offer is that they can be used in your IRA, SEP, or Keogh plan—plans that defer taxes on earnings.

But remember, unlike Treasury bills, notes, and bonds, corporate bonds are not guaranteed or backed by the government. Corporate bond issuers can and have defaulted. Your protection is the financial strength of the corporation. And the greater the financial strength of the issuer, the lower the coupon or interest rate because safety is traded off for lower yields.

֍ **Hint** If you live in a high-tax state, factor in the tax advantage of Treasury issues when considering corporate bonds. Income earned on Treasuries is subject to federal income tax but not state and local taxes.

A Corporate Bond Portfolio

- AT&T 7⅛ percent coupon, due 2002
- Beverly Entertainment 9⅛ percent coupon, due 2004

- Commonwealth Edison 8.75 percent coupon, due 2005
- Dow Chemical 8.5 percent coupon, due 2005
- Bell Tel of PA 8.25 percent coupon, due 2017

🔆 **Hint** The owner of these bonds will receive his or her return of principal staggered over three different years, starting in 2002 and ending in 2017. This technique, called **laddering**, can also be done with CDs. It is particularly effective for meeting college tuition bills, retirement needs, or other specific financial goals.

Corporate Bond Mutual Funds

As we mentioned above, with $5,000 you can buy only five bonds, and thus shares in a corporate bond mutual fund is a wiser choice. In a mutual fund you will own a proportionate part of a larger number of bonds, and the portfolio is professionally managed.

Three suggestions:
- Fidelity Short Term Bond Fund: 800-544-8888 and www.fidelity.com
- T. Rowe Price Short Term Bond: 800-638-5660 and www.troweprice.com
- Vanguard Short Term Bond Fund: 800-662-7447 and www.vanguard.com

Municipal Bonds

Municipal bonds, also known as tax-exempts, are a good choice for anyone in the 28 percent or higher tax brackets. "Munis," as they are called on Wall Street, are issued by cities, counties, states, and special agencies to finance various projects. Their biggest plus: Interest paid is exempt from federal income tax and, to residents of the area where issued, state and local taxes.

✋ **Caution** Two tax traps: 1. If you buy municipals outside the state where you are a resident, their interest incomes will be subject to taxes in your state. 2. Any capital gains made when you sell municipals is subject to all federal and most state tax laws.

Because of their tax advantage, municipal bonds pay lower interest rates than comparable corporate bonds or government securities.

The major retail brokers such as Merrill Lynch, Paine Webber, and others are primarily interested in working with customers who have a minimum of $15,000 to $25,000 to invest in these bonds.

Corporate Bonds

FOR WHOM
- Anyone seeking high fixed income who also accepts the risk of changing interest rates.
- Best for those who can hold their bonds until maturity in order to get back the bond's full face value.

SAFETY FACTOR
- Can be determined by bond ratings with AAA and AA being the highest.
- Varies depending upon the corporate issuer.
- Are not insured or guaranteed.

MINIMUM INVESTMENT
- $1,000 (many brokers have a $5,000 minimum).

ADVANTAGES
- Corporate bonds almost always pay higher interest rates than government bonds or those issued by municipalities.
- You can select bonds to come due when you need an influx of cash.
- A sound way to get a steady stream of income.

DISADVANTAGES
- Many bonds have call provisions.
- If you sell before maturity you may get back less than you paid.

- Interest income is subject to federal, state, and local taxes.
- There is generally minimum appreciation of your principal, whereas with many stocks, investors benefit from significant increases in the price of their shares.

Although you may indeed find a regular broker or a discount one who will take smaller orders, the commission will be hefty vis-à-vis your dollar investment. And markups on munis sold through brokers range from 1 to 4 percent.

So, if you have $15,000, invest instead by purchasing a unit investment trust or municipal bond fund, explained below.

Tips for Selecting Tax-Exempt Bonds

There are three factors to check when considering tax-exempt bonds: safety, yield, and liquidity. You can check the safety of any bond, tax-exempt or not, through Moody's or Standard & Poor's rating services.

Safety

In addition to sticking to A-rated bonds, you can increase your safety factor by purchasing bonds that are insured even though their yields are slightly lower than uninsured munis. Because municipal bond issuers have occasionally defaulted—the best known example being the Washington Public Power System—insured bonds are a sound idea in today's economic climate.

In order to insure a bond, the issuer pays an insurance company a premium that ranges from 0.1 percent to 2 percent of the bond's total principal and interest. The insurance company agrees to pay both the principal and the interest to bondholders if the issuer defaults on making payment. Policies generally last the life of the bond. Your broker can tell you which bonds are insured. For additional information on insured municipal bonds, write to:

AMBAC Indemnity Corp.
1 State Street Plaza
New York, NY 10004
212-668-0340
www.ambac.com

Yield

The second factor in municipal bond selection is yield. Tax-exempts, as we mentioned before, pay lower interest rates than most taxable bonds, and therefore are not appropriate for people in low tax brackets or for placement in already tax-deferred retirement accounts, such as an IRA. Yet for investors in high tax brackets, municipal bonds can reap surprisingly good returns.

If, for example, you are married, file a joint return, and earn $45,000 annually, you need a yield of 10.76 percent on a taxable investment such as a corporate bond to equal a 7.75 percent tax-exempt yield. The chart on page 119 shows the relationship between taxed and tax-free income.

-ᗧ- **Hint** You can further boost your return by investing in triple-exempt municipals—those in which interest is free from federal, state, and local taxes for residents. Triple-exempts are especially good for people living in states with high income taxes.

Liquidity

The third factor involved in municipal bond selection is liquidity—that is, the ability to find someone who wants to buy your bond, should you wish to sell before maturity. It is best to stick with bonds of large, well-known municipalities or state governments. If you want to sell an obligation of the Moorland Iowa School District, for example, it may be weeks before you find a dealer willing to buy these obscure bonds.

Note: Municipal bond mutual funds are also very liquid.

Types of Municipal Bonds

- **General obligation bonds (GOs)** are the safest category of munis. Sold to help build roads, schools, and government buildings, they are tax-exempt as long as no more than 10 percent of their proceeds goes to a private enterprise. Bonds issued for nonprofit organizations are also tax-exempt. GOs have the highest safety ratings because they are backed by the issuer's full taxing and revenue-raising powers.
- **Revenue bonds** depend upon the income earned by a specific project or authority, such as road or bridge tolls, or revenues from a publicly financed hospital.
- **Industrial development bonds** are issued to finance facilities that are in turn leased to private corporations. The tax law stipulates that if more than 10 percent of the proceeds raised by their sale is used by private enterprise, the interest a bondholder receives may be subject to a special tax, known as the alternative minimum tax (AMT). The AMT is designed to make sure that Americans with tax-sheltered investments do not escape paying income taxes.

🖐 **Caution** Before investing in an industrial development bond, check with your accountant to see if you are subject to the AMT. If so, avoid these particular bonds.

🔆 **Hint** Zero coupon municipals are an excellent way to save for a child's education. They are sold at a discount and redeemed in the future at a higher face value. And you never have to pay federal income tax on them. Zeros are explained in full at the end of this chapter.

Municipal Bond Mutual Funds and Unit Investment Trusts

As you know, putting all your eggs in one basket is not sound planning. As a hedge against the risk of an issuer defaulting, it's wise to hold at least five to ten different bonds and/or buy only insured bonds.

Here are three reasonably priced ways to own a diversified muni bond portfolio with just $5,000. In all three, your risk is spread out through participation in large, diversified portfolios of bonds that are professionally selected.

Municipal Bond Mutual Funds

A municipal bond fund's portfolio is made up of tax-exempt munis; most hold over 100 bonds. The typical minimum investment is $1,000. They operate like any other mutual fund. The portfolio manager buys and sells securities in order to maximize the fund's yield. Unlike a unit investment trust (explained below) in which the yield is fixed, a mutual fund's shares fluctuate on a daily basis.

Interest earned is automatically reinvested unless you give directions to the contrary, and an increasing number of bond funds allow you to write checks, usually a minimum of $500, against the value of your shares.

If you ever wish to sell, the fund will buy back your shares at the current market price.

Tax-Exempt Unit Investment Trusts

For those who wish to lock in a fixed tax-exempt yield, a unit investment trust is ideal. Most require a minimum investment of $1,000 per unit. These prepackaged, diversified portfolios lock in a specific, unchanging yield. Unlike bond mutual funds, they are "unmanaged," and once the bonds for the trust have been selected, no new issues are added. (Issues that turn out to be a problem, however, can be sold in order to minimize losses.) The trust gradually liquidates itself as the bonds mature.

Four Municipal Bond Mutual Funds

Alliance Municipal Insured National: 800-221-5672 and www.alliancecapital.com

American Century Intermediate Term Tax Free: 800-345-2021 and www.americancentury.com

---

Nuveen Tax-Exempt Limited Term: 800-227-4648 and www.nuveen.com

Vanguard Muni High Yield: 800-662-7447 and www. vanguard.com

Unit investment trusts are set up by big brokerage houses and bond dealers who buy several million dollars worth of bonds and then sell them to individual investors in $1,000 pieces. You pay the broker a onetime up-front fee, commonly 4.5 percent. You also pay trustee fees of up to .2 percent a year.

A typical unit investment trust holds 20 bonds until maturity, unless the bonds are called or defaulted. Most hold bonds maturing in 25 to 30 years, though some are set up to end sooner, and you can buy them with shorter maturities in the secondary market.

Note: While you own a trust, you receive tax-free income on a monthly or quarterly basis.

-ϙ̇- **Hint** Don't be surprised if your checks are not the same every month. As bonds mature or are called, this activity is reflected in your monthly checks.

If you do not wish to hold the trust until maturity, you can sell it in the secondary market either to the sponsor or to another broker. What you get back will depend on the market. If interest rates have fallen, you will get more; but if they've gone up, it's possible that you may not even get back your original price.

🖐 **Caution** Unit investment trusts are not as liquid as mutual funds.

Talk to your broker in order to find out which trusts are available now, and at what price. Be certain to check the rating of the bonds held in trust. For tops in safety or if you're conservative, stick with AAA-rated bonds or buy an insured trust.

Single-State Investment Trusts and Bond Funds
These are a good investment if you live in a high income tax state.

Both single-state investment trusts and single-state bond funds contain bonds that have a triple tax exemption—that is, free from federal, state, and local taxes for residents of the issuing state.

Trusts are sold by regional brokers, large brokerage firms, and bond specialists. In addition, two companies sponsor a number of single-state trusts. Contact them for further information:

- John Nuveen
  800-227-4648
  www.nuveen.com
- Van Kampen
  800-225-2222
  www.vankampen.com

Single-state muni mutual bond funds are sold by the mutual fund company in the case of no-load funds and by stockbrokers in the case of load funds. Among the leading no-loads with single-state muni funds are:

- American Century
- Dreyfus
- Fidelity
- T. Rowe Price
- Scudder
- Vanguard

🖐 **Caution** Single-state muni bond funds obviously lack the diversity of a broadly based national municipal bond fund. If you live in a state with fiscal problems, put no more than one-third of your tax-free portfolio in single-state mutual funds or unit investment trusts.

The Tax-Exempt Edge

Find your tax bracket on the left, then at the top of the table find the tax-exempt yield. Read down to determine the yield you need on a taxable security to equal the yield on a municipal.

	Tax-Exempt Yield			
Tax bracket	6.5%	7%	7.5%	8%
15%	7.64	8.23	8.82	9.41
28%	9.02	9.72	10.41	11.11
33%	9.7	10.45	11.19	11.94

Zero Coupon Bonds

If you will need money for college tuition, retirement, or to meet some other long-term financial goal, zero coupon bonds offer a viable solution. You make a small investment initially and get a large balloon payment in the future.

How Zeros Work

A zero, unlike regular bonds, pays no interest until maturity. To compensate, it is sold at a deep discount, well below the $1,000 standard bond price, and it increases in value at a compound rate so that by maturity it is worth much more than when you bought it. Although this type of bond does not pay interest along the way, you will be taxed annually by the IRS as though it did.

Let's look at an example: A $1,000 zero yielding 6.2 percent matures in 20 years. It's selling for only $85.40. You pay $85.40. Your $85.40 earns 6.2 percent but you don't receive your investment payments. Instead, they're reinvested and earn 6.2 percent as well. After 20 years, your $84.50 will equal $1,000. Interest turns into principal and is paid to you in a lump sum upon maturity.

Note: EE savings bonds are zeros.

As you can see, with a zero coupon bond you know ahead of time exactly how much money you will have when the bond comes due on a given date.

The Two Types of Zeros

There are two types of popular zeros: U.S. Treasury zeros or muni zeros. The first are issued by the U.S. Treasury while munis are issued by municipalities, states, and other agencies. There are also a handful of corporate zeros, but they are very rare.

Zero Coupon Bonds

FOR WHOM
- Those who know they will need a certain amount of money at a certain time in the future.
- Those who can hold bonds until maturity because zeros fluctuate widely in price.

MINIMUM
- Typically between $150 and $450, but varies widely.

SAFETY FACTOR
- Minimal risk.

ADVANTAGES
- You know precisely how much you must invest now to a get a certain dollar amount on a certain date in the future.

- You do not have to be concerned with the reinvestment of interest payments as is the case with regular bonds.

DISADVANTAGES
- Yields are a half to one percentage point below ordinary bonds.
- The IRS insists that taxes be paid annually on zero coupon bonds just as if you had actually received the interest.
- You are paying taxes on theoretical interest even though no cash is received until the date of maturity.

A Stock Portfolio for Beginners

Buy stocks that go up, and if they don't, don't buy 'em.
—Will Rogers

Easier said than done. Yet even though stocks go down as well as up, many Americans like owning stocks, owning a piece of American industry. Many actually do more than just think about it—over 28 percent of the U.S. population owns stocks.

There are four compelling reasons why at the $5,000 level, you too should consider buying stocks:

- Over the long term, stocks outperform bonds and Treasuries.
- Stocks offer the possibility of price appreciation.
- Stocks offer the possibility of keeping ahead of inflation.
- Stocks, especially those paying high dividends, are also a source of income.

🔆 **Hint** If you have never owned a stock, read "What Exactly Is a Stock?" in Chapter 8.

Are You Ready for the Market?

Prior to selecting stocks for your own portfolio, you must have money set aside for an emergency. At least three months' worth of living expenses should be safely stashed away in a liquid investment, such as a money market mutual fund, a money market deposit account, or a certificate of deposit. Once this has been accomplished and you have accumulated $5,000, you're ready to go.

Although it is possible to invest in the market with smaller amounts of money, in order to establish a truly diversified portfolio you need a base of about $5,000. (**See** Chapter 8 for information on Mini-Investor Plans.)

First determine your investment goals. Are you seeking a stock that pays a high cash dividend, or would you prefer to buy one that will appreciate substantially in price? Do you want liquidity—that is, the ability to get money back when you want it—or are you content to wait for long-term growth? Your goals make a difference, because no one stock offers high dividends, instant liquidity, spectacular appreciation, plus stability.

The Risk Factor

Before you invest, keep in mind that while many stocks are profitable investments and return handsome rewards in terms of capital appreciation, they can also decline in price. There is no guarantee that you will make a profit. Careful selection is essential.

The ABCs of Stock Selection

As you recall from Chapter 8, a **common stock** is a fractional share of ownership in a corporation. For example, if a corporation has one million outstanding shares and you buy one share, you then own one-millionth of that corporation.

This ownership enables you to participate in the fortunes of the corporation. If the corporation prospers, its earnings (which are expressed as earnings per share) will rise, which in turn tends to make the price of the stock rise. Simply put, the corporation's value has increased. Often, a portion of these earnings is shared with stockholders in the form of a cash dividend that is paid out four times a year.

If you believe that certain corporations or industries will flourish in the coming years, try selecting several common stocks in these areas as an investment for income, growth, or a combination of the two.

🔆 **Hint** You might want to follow this rule of thumb, especially at the outset. Don't put more than 10 percent of your money into the stock of any one company and no more than 20 percent in any one industry.

Remember that stocks can also decline in price and you should try to confine your selections primarily to blue-chip companies; that is, large, well-financed, and established corporations with secure positions within their industry.

Here are five key standards to use in judging a stock.

1. **Earnings per share should show an upward trend over the previous five years.** If, however, earnings declined for one year out of five, this is acceptable, provided the overall trend continues to rise.

Earnings per share, simply defined, is the company's net income (after taxes and money for preferred stock dividends) divided by the average number of common stock shares outstanding. You will find it listed in the company's annual report or in professional materials such as *Value Line* or Standard & Poor's *Stock Guide*, available at your library or in any broker's office.

2. **Increasing earnings should be accompanied by similarly increasing dividends.** You should study the cash dividend payments over the previous five-year period. In some cases a corporation will use most of its earnings to invest in future growth and dividends may be quite modest, and rightly so. But even in these cases, some token dividend should be paid annually. Ideally, a company should earn at least $5 for every $4 it pays out.

In conjunction with the company's dividend, you should note its **yield**, which is the current dividend divided by the price of a share. It is listed in the newspaper along with the dividend and other statistics. The yield should be higher for a stock you purchase for income than for one selected for potential price appreciation (see sample stock listing, later in this chapter).

3. **Standard & Poor's rates each company's financial strength.** For you, the $5,000 investor, the minimum acceptable rating should be A.

4. **The number of outstanding shares should be at least 10 million.** Marketability and liquidity depend upon a large supply of common stock shares. Ten million shares ensures activity by the major institutions, such as mutual funds, pension funds, and insurance companies. Institutional participation helps guarantee an active market in which you and others can readily buy and sell the company's stock.

5. **Study the company's price to earnings ratio (P/E ratio).** This ratio is found by dividing the previous year's earnings per share (or the current year's estimated earnings) into the current price of the stock. The **P/E ratio** is one of the most important analytical tools in the business. It reflects investor opinion about the stock and about the market as a whole. For example, a P/E of 11 means investors are willing to pay 11 times earnings for that stock. A P/E of 11 indicates greater investor interest and confidence than a P/E of 7 or 5.

A P/E ratio under 10 is considered conservative, and, depending upon the company, its industry, and your broker's advice, you can feel comfortable with a P/E of 10 or less. As a company's P/E moves above 10, you begin to pay a premium for some aspect of the company's future.

Yet a P/E ratio above 10 may very well be justified by outstanding prospects for future growth, by new technological advances, or by worldwide shortages of a product that the company produces.

Basically, the P/E ratio is the measure of the common stock's value to investors. A low P/E of 5 or 6 usually means that the prospects are clouded by uncertainty. Similarly, a P/E of 14 or 15 indicates a keen appetite on the part of investors to participate in that company's future.

⚡ **Hint** Whatever stock or stocks you decide to buy, you want to get in at the lowest possible P/E—before there is a lot of investor interest and the P/E is bid up. No one can say exactly what ratio you should accept, and it is here that your selection process and your broker's advice become important.

How to Read a Financial Page

Once you own stocks, you will want to know how they are doing—whether they are going up or down in price. To find out, you can read the market quotations in the daily newspaper.

You will find your stock listed under the name of its exchange—the New York Stock Exchange, American Stock Exchange, or Nasdaq. Here's how it works, using Gannett as an example.

52 Week				Yld		Sales				
High	Low	Stock	Div	%	P/E	100s	High	Low	Last	Chg
79.60	53.00	Gannett	.96	1.3	20	59543	71.97	66.75	71.30	+1.04

- The first two columns give the **highest and lowest prices** per share for the last 52 weeks. In the case of Gannett, the high was $79.60 and the low, $53.00. *Note:* If there has been a new high or a new low, you will see an arrow pointing up or down right next to the name of the stock.

- The next column gives the **name of the stock,** sometimes in abbreviated form.

- Then comes the current **annual dividend,** if any, given in dollars. Gannett is paying a dividend of $0.96/share.

- This is followed by the **dividend yield,** given as a percentage. To determine the yield, divide the dividend by the closing price. Gannett's yield is 1.3%.

- The **Price/Earnings ratio** is next. It is determined by dividing the price of the stock by the earnings per share (eps) over the last quarter. The eps figure is not given in the tables. Gannett's P/E is 20.

- **Sales** (sometimes listed as **Vol**), refers to the volume of shares traded the previous day. Unless the letter **z** appears before this number, multiply by 100 to get the actual number of shares. If there's a **z,** do not multiply by 100 because the actual number of shares traded is given. *Note:* If the information is underlined, it indicates an unusually large volume for that day.

- **High** refers to the highest price traded during the previous day. Sometime during the previous day, Gannett traded as high as $71.97.

- **Low** refers to the lowest price traded during the previous day. Sometime during the previous day, Gannett traded as low as $66.75.

- **Last** refers to the final trade of the previous day, which for Gannett was $71.30.
- **Change** refers to the difference between today's closing price and the previous day's closing price. A minus (–) indicates that the price fell. A plus (+) indicates the price rose. Gannett's shares rose $1.04. If there's no plus or minus sign, then the closing price was the same as the day before. If the price has changed 5% or more, it will be printed in boldface.

Note: These figures do not include the broker's commission.

Buying Stocks

Once you have decided to become involved with the stock market, the next issue to resolve is whether to use a broker or to select your own stocks. Generally speaking, if you have never owned a stock before, it is probably more prudent to get help from an experienced professional than to go it alone.

On the other hand, you could join an investment club (see Chapter 9) or pick hometown stocks (see Chapter 13) and very likely be quite successful.

Selecting a Broker

Knowing when and how to seek the advice of an expert is a critical part of being a successful investor. If you've never had a broker (or if you've had one you did not like) you can find the right one by doing some investigative work well in advance. Plan on spending three to four weeks to locate the broker who is right for you.

Start by thinking about how you selected your doctor or lawyer. Someone else probably suggested them to you. Getting the recommendations of friends and colleagues whose judgment you respect is one of the best ways to find a good broker. Ask your boss, accountant, banker, uncle, or doctor if they have a broker they like.

After gathering several names, call and make appointments with each one. Tell them the amount of money you have to invest. Not all brokers are interested in small accounts, yet many are. Those who are realize that a small account obviously has the potential of becoming a larger one over time. A number of online brokers are willing to open small accounts. You will also find that reliable regional brokers are prepared to handle accounts of all sizes, and they are eager to help local investors.

If you feel you don't need investment advice, you can save on commissions by buying through a "discount" broker, such as Charles Schwab, Quick & Reilly, Muriel Siebert, and Olde. In either event, a broker must execute the final buy or sell transaction for you.

Before you interview your broker candidates, prepare a list of questions to ask them. It should include these four items, plus anything else that concerns you:

1. *Do you handle accounts of this size?* You definitely don't want to use a broker who is uninterested in $5,000.

2. *Can you give me one or two references?* Skip over any broker who says no.

3. *How long have you been a broker?* Any broker tends to look great in a good market. You want an experienced person who knows how to handle money in bad times as well as good.

4. *How should I invest my $5,000?* Beware of the broker who advises you to put it all in one stock, or even all in the market. Unless you have specifically said the total amount is to be invested in stocks, the broker should advise you to diversify.

Going It Alone
Once you have gained some feeling for the market, you may want to plunge right in and do your own stock selection.

The best way to minimize risk, of course, is to be well informed. To be your own broker you must be prepared to spend a significant amount of time reading about the economy and about individual companies, as well as about the major industries.

Finding Top-Notch Information

- **Specialized financial periodicals and newspapers** are excellent sources of information on the general economic climate and the stock market. In particular, among the newspapers: *Barron's*, the *Wall Street Journal*, the *New York Times*, and the *Chicago Tribune*. Good magazines are: *Forbes, Business Week, Bottom Line, Fortune, U.S. News & World Report*, and *Money*.

  The money section of *USA Today* is excellent for beginners, as is *Better Investing*, the monthly magazine of the National Association of Investment Corps. Devoted to investment education, it analyzes stocks and covers various views on investments (**see** Chapter 9).

- **Brokerage firms** have a wealth of research material. The large houses will send you some material, even if you are not a customer—at least for a limited period. Many have copies of newsletters on display in their retail offices. Although much of this information is generally known, you can still gather ideas, and certainly it is valuable for background data.

- **Annual reports of corporations** are an important source. Write or call any company you are considering investing in and ask for a copy.

- **Standard & Poor's** *Stock Reports* is regarded as a bible in the financial world. It covers each company listed on the NYSE. S&P also publishes similar volumes for the American Stock Exchange and for over-the-counter stocks. The material is revised periodically. For each corporation you will find a summary description, the current outlook, and new developments, plus a ten-year statistical table.

- **Standard & Poor's** *Stock Guide* is a small monthly booklet containing basic data in condensed form on 10,000 stocks: price range, P/E ratio, dividend history, sales, an abbreviated balance sheet, earnings, and the S&P rating. A similar monthly booklet is put out covering bonds. For further details on all S&P publications, contact:

  Standard and Poor's Corporation
  800-221-5277
  www.standardandpoors.com

- **Value Line Investment Survey** contains the most comprehensive coverage of stocks. Value Line follows 1,700 companies and their industries. Each industry is updated quarterly. Stocks are ranked on the basis of timeliness for purchase and safety. A subscription to this service also includes a separate weekly analysis of the market and general economic situation plus an in-depth discussion of one stock recommended for purchase. Contact:

  Value Line, Inc.
  800-833-0046
  www.valueline.com

- **Financial newsletters can be helpful**, but they vary enormously in reliability and success as far as their advice goes. Before subscribing to any newsletter, try to locate copies at your library or by contacting the publisher. Many will send a free copy or offer trial subscriptions at a reduced rate.

☀ **Hint** There is also a service that rates the advisers. *Hulbert Financial Digest* is a monthly newsletter that tracks 160 stock market newsletters based on their performance in recommending stocks. One issue is free; a year's subscription is $59. Contact:

Hulbert Financial Digest
5051 Backlick Road
Annandale, VA 22003
888-HULBERT
www.hulbertdigest.com

- **Insider trading.** The sale and purchase of a company's stock by officials of the corporation is one way to determine trends in the price of the stock. This information is given in *Value Line*.

Your Investment Achilles' Heel

Even with rational research and thoughtful planning on your part, you may still fall prey to one or more of the ubiquitous emotional traps that lie in wait in the investment field.

A Beginner's Portfolio

20 GROWTH STOCKS TO CONSIDER

Abbott Laboratories	Harley-Davidson
Bank of New York	Hormel
Bob Evans Farms	Pep Boys
Bristol-Myers Squibb	PepsiCo
Clorox	Procter & Gamble
Daktronics	St. Jude Medical
Exxon-Mobil	Smucker's
Flextronics	Tootsie Roll
General Electric	Walgreen
Gillette	Wrigley

The Smarty's Six-Step Game Plan

1. **Figure out whether you're investing for income or for long-term appreciation.** Then select stocks that match your goal.

2. When you're investing long term, remember that the market fluctuates by the minute.

   Focus on earnings, not on daily prices.

3. **Know something about the industry.** Don't purchase a medical technology stock or a high-tech issue if you don't know about medical technology or high tech.

4. **Read the company's annual and quarterly reports** before buying its stock. You wouldn't buy a car without a test drive.

5. **Stick with companies** if they are leaders within their industry.

6. **Be patient.** Think long term, but sell when you've doubled your money.

Every investor has areas of vulnerability. If you recognize yours, it's possible to eliminate many errors and reduce misjudgments. Here are the five most common pitfalls you should avoid when buying and selling stocks.

1. **Holding on to securities too long,** hoping a poor performer will turn out to be a winner. It's rare; learn when to give up.

2. **Reacting immediately to negative news** and selling too soon. Think about it overnight, then respond.

3. **Refusing to sell** and take profits because you feel you can squeeze out a few more points. This is known as greed; resist it.

4. **Refusing to take a profit** because of capital gains tax, even when the stock is fully valued. This is silly, if not stupid.

5. **Hanging on to a stock** you inherited because of sentimental feelings. Really! Stocks have no feelings.

To avoid these five pitfalls, and others, you should set up a smart game plan—based on knowing what your financial objectives are and then sticking to them. Read on . . .

PART SIX
OVER THE TOP

Now that you've read this far, you should be feeling pretty good—you've got more than $5,000 burning a hole in your pocket. As your assets grow, so do your investment options and your ability to assume a bit more risk. And with greater risk often come greater returns. But take care not to go overboard. Keep your original investment goals in mind and adhere to them.

In this section we'll take a look at REITs and foreign stocks and bonds, and how to invest a windfall.

REITs

Investing in real estate stocks and mutual funds, like any other market industry, comes with a degree of risk. Yet over the years, REITs (Real Estate Investment Trusts) have made money for many investors.

REITs are like mutual funds—they own a variety of properties or mortgages on properties. Their shares trade on the stock exchanges. While some are high in risk, many are considered relatively sound investments, offering an easier way to participate in commercial real estate than by directly owning property, such as an office building or rental apartment house.

REITs were created by Congress in 1960 to give individuals a way to invest in commercial real estate. They have a unique tax structure. They avoid taxation as long as they pay out 95 percent of their income to shareholders—which they do in the form of dividends. That's good news for you as an investor because the dividends tend to be high.

REITs frequently focus on specific geographical areas and/or on particular types of property, such as shopping centers, commercial buildings, storage units, or health care facilities.

Recently REITs in health care and self storage have been the strongest performers.

In addition to consulting with your stockbroker, before adding a REIT to your portfolio read the evaluations in *Value Line Investment Survey*, a weekly research service. Value Line has several analysts who specialize in studying 20 different REITs. Stick with those that have a ranking of 3 or better for both safety and timeliness.

Six REITs to Consider

Name	Yield
BRE Properties	6.5 %
Health Care Property	8.4
New Plan Excel	8.9
Thornburg Mortgage	9.5
Washington REIT	5.6
Weingarten Realty	6.6

(Source: *Value Line Investment Survey*)

Foreign Stocks and Bonds

There is an investment world beyond America. And the electronic age has made the flow of money and information instantaneous, so whatever happens on the Hong Kong stock exchange or to the price of gold in London has a direct impact on investors in Des Moines, Duluth, and Detroit.

It is important to consider foreign investments for many reasons, among them the fact that two-thirds of the total value of the world's stock markets is outside the U.S.

Therefore if you invest only in the U.S., you're missing many opportunities and at various times, some of the best-managed and fastest-growing companies.

U.S. Multinational Companies

American multinationals—companies with at least 40 percent of earnings and profits derived from foreign business—make it possible to invest overseas while still sitting at home. Here are 15 of the many U.S. blue-chip corporations that fall into this category:

Abbott Laboratories
Avon Products
Black & Decker
Bristol-Myers Squibb
Coca-Cola
Colgate-Palmolive
Exxon-Mobil
General Electric
Gillette
IBM
McDonald's
Microsoft
PepsiCo
Procter & Gamble
Wrigley

Using Mutual Funds

I recommend that you begin investing in foreign stocks and bonds through a mutual fund until you become thoroughly experienced. Start by studying the various no-load funds offered by these companies.

Fidelity
Franklin Templeton
Scudder
T. Rowe Price
Vanguard

American Depository Receipts

Another way to invest overseas is through American Depository Receipts (ADRs). ADRs are negotiable receipts that represent ownership of shares in a foreign corporation that is traded in an American securities market.

ADRs are issued by an American bank but the actual shares are held by a foreign depository bank or agent. This custodian is usually but not always an office of the American bank.

With ADRs you can buy, sell, or hold the foreign stock without actually taking physical posession of it. They are registered by the SEC and sold by stockbrokers. You pay for them in U.S. dollars and you receive any dividends in dollars.

Here are 15 popular ADRs:

Amway Japan
Barclays Bank
British Airways
British Petroleum
British Telecom
Cable & Wireless
Glaxco Holding
Honda Motor
Hong Kong Telecom
Korea Electric Power
NewsCorp., Ltd.
Shell Transport
SmithKline Beecham
Tele Danmark
Unilever

Purchasing ADRs Directly

A growing number of foreign companies are offering direct purchase plans for their ADRs, enabling you to buy them just as you would a U.S. stock.

- The Bank of New York's program Global BuyDirect at: 800-345-1612 or: www.bankofny.com/adr
- J.P. Morgan's Global Invest Direct at: 800-997-8970 or: www.adr.com

Among the ADRs available through these programs:

Bank of Ireland
Cadbury Schweppes
Durban Roodeport Deep
Fila
General Cable

Grupo Industrial Durango
Randgold
Rank Group Royal Dutch
Sony
TDK

Investing a Windfall

Perhaps this year you'll win the Powerball lottery or get a big bonus at work or an unexpected inheritance from your aunt in Peoria. Windfalls also come from legal and court settlements, buyouts, separation packages, stock options, retirement plans, and divorce decrees. And while it's perfectly wonderful to spend some of it (no more than 5 to 6 percent, please!) on a gourmet wine and food tour of France or a new SUV, it's equally important not to blow it all.

A study by a group of certified financial planners found that 90 percent of the people who come into a windfall spent all of their money within five years. I want you to be among the 10 percent, not the 90 percent. A windfall offers you a great opportunity to create a financial cushion and give you peace of mind.

What to do

Step 1. Do nothing at first. Get used to the idea that your net worth is greater than it was a month ago. Don't go on a spending spree. People often have unrealistic ideas of how much money they really have. If you quit your job or take up life in the fast lane, you may not be able to sustain yourself.

STEP 2. **Split up the money.** Don't put more than $100,000 in one bank—that's the cap on FDIC insurance. (see page 11). Divide your windfall among a money fund, bank CDs, and short-term Treasuries until you devise a long-term plan.

STEP 3. **List your immediate needs.** Money from a court settlement, for example, may be needed to pay medical bills or used to live on because of a disabling injury or a death of a breadwinner. If you've gone heavily in debt, getting rid of that debt should be at the top of your list. If you don't have adequate health and liability insurance, put that on the list. But make certain you don't turn right around and go wild with the plastic.

STEP 4. **List your secondary goals.** This is the fun part. Maybe you'd like to pay off your mortgage, buy a house, take a vacation, set up a scholarship at your old alma mater, buy a Harley. But just list these things . . . don't take any action yet.

STEP 5. **Call your accountant.** Before investing or spending your windfall, set aside enough money to cover taxes. A large windfall is likely to push you into a higher tax bracket.

STEP 6. **Check your emotions and those of others.** Keep cool. Don't lose your head. Don't freeze. Don't panic. People are rarely emotionally prepared for this type of event. Some people feel a bit guilty about receiving money they didn't earn. Others feel overwhelmed. Some pretend it never happened. People's reactions are all over the place—yours and those of your friends. You may find that relatives you never heard of will come out of the woodwork and ask for help. People you work with may suddenly be resentful. Think before you react. Don't let your emotions or those of anyone else rule.

STEP 7. **Watch out for scams.** If you've won a pile of money you will be besieged with "get-rich-quick" schemes. Resist each and every one.

STEP 8. **Update your will.** Having more money means having an up-to-date will.

STEP 8. **Use a professional.** Call your attorney and/or financial adviser. You can probably handle investing a small amount of money. But if you're dealing with thousands or millions, get advice from people who are in the business of handling thousands or millions. Invest gradually, allocating the money to different stocks, bonds, or mutual funds. Keep in mind that conservative accounts rarely exceed 60 percent in stocks.

🔆 **Hint** If you decide to be a do-it-yourself investor, see Chapter 16 on index funds and perhaps put half your windfall in the S&P 500, 25 percent in small caps, and 20 percent in international stocks and bonds. And what do you do with the remaining 5 percent? That's the part you get to blow on something wild and wonderful.

Think a windfall is unlikely? Think again. Government figures show that inheritances will reach $340 billion a year by the year 2015. So be very careful with the largest check you may ever receive!

APPENDICES

A. Nine Easy and Painless Ways to Save

B. Ten Steps Toward College Tuition

C. Scams, Swindles, and Suckers

D. The Top 25 Financial Websites

E. If You're Fired

F. Cash in a Flash: 10 Sources of Instant Money

G. Your Next Steps

Nine Easy and Painless Ways to Save

Granted, it's much more fun to spend money on a romantic restaurant dinner or on a Caribbean vacation than to save your pennies or dollars. Yet to make certain you can always dine out and travel in style, you do need to save.

Extra dollars not only make dreams come true, they also let you sleep at night. If you want college for your kids, a house of your own, and a retirement nest egg, then build your savings by following these nine easy tips. You'll find saving is infectious.

1. **Make savings your first bill.** Once a month when you pay your bills, write a check to deposit in your money market fund or savings account at your bank or credit union. Start by saving 1 percent of your take-home pay the first month; then increase the amount by 1 percent each month. By the end of the year you'll be socking away 12 percent a year.

2. **Use automatic savings plans.** If you don't see it, you won't spend it. Arrange for a certain amount—it can be as little as $50—to be taken out of your paycheck and automatically transferred to your savings or money market fund at a bank or credit union. Ask if your

employer also has an automatic plan for **EE Savings Bonds.** Alternatives: Have your bank automatically transfer a certain amount from checking to savings each month; or have a mutual fund automatically withdraw money from your checking account and put it into its highest yielding money fund.

3. **Leave credit cards at home.** Pay with cash or by check. You'll spend less and you'll avoid those whopping monthly interest charges on unpaid credit card balances.

4. **Defer taxes.** Money in an IRA, Keogh, 401(k), or other qualified retirement plan grows tax-free until withdrawn. You can fund these plans by making small contributions several times a year rather than by trying to pay in one large lump sum. Alternatives: Buy investments that are fully or partially tax-exempt: municipal bonds, municipal bond mutual funds, EE Savings Bonds, and U.S. Treasury securities. (But don't put them in your retirement plan.)

5. **Contribute to a stock purchase plan.** Many companies allow employees to contribute part of their salary to buy the firm's stock through automatic payroll deductions.

6. **Reinvest stock dividends. See** page 46 for details.

7. **Keep making payments.** When you've paid off a mortgage or a loan, continue to write a check for the same amount (or at least half the amount) every month and put it into savings. You've learned to live without that money, so now you can sock it away.

8. **Save your change at the end of the day.** Small amounts add up quickly. Put your nickels, dimes, and quarters in a jar before going to bed. Better bet: Save one-dollar bills.

9. **Treat yourself.** Saving is smart but not always immediately gratifying. The payoff is sometimes several years away. So spend a little on yourself now and then. It will make saving much easier.

I'd like to leave you with these final words of wisdom from the great mystery writer, Agatha Christie: "Where large sums of money are concerned, it's advisable to trust nobody."

The same is true of small sums, from $50 to $5,000. And now that you've read this book, you are well armed to trust yourself when it comes to things financial.

Ten Steps Toward College Tuition

You know college is going to be an expensive proposition, whether your child or grandchild goes to an Ivy League school or to a more reasonably priced state university. There's no need to panic, but on the other hand, there is a need to do something. In fact, there may be several somethings.

Here are ten steps to help you get headed in the right direction.

1. **Call T. Rowe Price** and get a free copy of "The College Planning Kit." It's easy to follow and will help you determine how much money you need to set aside each month depending upon the age of your child. **Info:** 800-638-5660 or www.troweprice.com.

2. **Decide in whose name.** If you save funds in your child's name, the first $750 is tax free; the second $750 is taxed at the child's rate, which is most likely lower than yours. Then when your child turns fourteen all the child's investment income is taxed at the child's rate. (*Note*: These figures are continually adjusted.)

However, if college savings are in your name, your child is more likely to get financial aid. Schools ask parents to contribute 5.65 percent of their assets for each year's tuition but require a whopping 35 percent of the assets held in a child's name.

Best bet: Discuss with a knowledgeable accountant before making this decision.

3. **Stockpile EE savings bonds.** If you put the bonds in your name and use them to pay for tuition (not room and board), you will escape paying federal taxes on the income the bonds earn. (EE Bonds are exempt from state and local taxes for everyone. **See** Chapter 3.)

🖐 **Caution** This works only if your annual adjusted gross income falls below certain caps, currently $110,100 for married couples and $69,100 for single parents. However, these figures increase along with inflation. **Info:** 800-US-BONDS and www.savingsbonds.gov

4. **Fund your 401(k) plan.** This and other retirement plans often let you borrow up to 50 percent of the amount invested, or $50,000, whichever is less. The interest rate is typically prime plus one or two points and repayment is made through automatic payroll deductions back into your own account, not to a bank.

5. **Buy zero coupon bonds.** These are tailor-made for college accounts because you know exactly how much you'll get when the bonds mature. Sold at a deep discount, they pay no interest until maturity. For example, a ten-year zero Treasury bond selling for $530 will be worth $1,000 in the year 2005. (**See** Chapter 17.)

6. **Ladder back CDs and treasuries.** Buy a series of CDs and/or U.S. Treasuries timed to come due each fall as your child heads off to school. (**See** Chapters 7, 12, and 17.)

7. **Consider a mortarboard mutual fund.** Several mutual fund companies have no-load funds designed to help finance a child or grandchild's undergraduate degree. They typically buy growth stocks, often of companies children are familiar with. The funds also provide plenty of literature about investing and saving that kids can understand.

- American Century GiftTrust: 800-345-2021
- Monetta Express Children's Program: 800-MONETTA
- Stein Roe Young Investor Fund: 800-338-2550

8. **Start an Education IRA.** Anyone, related or not, can open this

type of account for a child. Up to $2,000 can be invested annually, until the child turns eighteen. There's no tax deduction for contributions, but the money and its earnings are tax free if used for qualified elementary, secondary, or college expenses before the child turns thirty. The contributor's AGI must fall within certain dollar amounts. For current caps: www.taxplanet.com. If the money has not been used by the time the beneficiary is thirty, it can be rolled over to another qualified family member, perhaps a younger brother or sister.

9. **Consider a state-sponsored 529 plan.** There are two types of 529s: prepaid tuition and a savings plan.

- With the prepaid, you lock in future tuition at a selected state college at today's rates. You do this by paying the bill in a lump sum or in installments.

- The savings trust, unlike the Education IRA, has no income limits for participation, although states impose varying caps on the total amount the account can hold. And anyone—parents, grandparents, other relatives and friends—can contribute.

    The money, typically invested in a mix of stocks, bonds, and/or mutual funds, accumulates tax deferred. When you take out money to pay for undergrad or graduate school, you do not pay any tax on the increased value of the account.

INFO: For details on your state's plan (each one differs slightly), go to www.collegesavings.org. Then, before proceeding, find out:

1. how the money is invested;
2. what the rate of return is;
3. if the money can be used for schools outside your state;
4. what happens if your child does not go to college;
5. if the beneficiary can be changed;
6. if you can deduct your contribution from your state income taxes;
7. if the money will reduce your child's chances of receiving financial aid.

💡 **Hint** If your state plan is not to your liking, nearly 20 of them, including Maine, Massachusetts, and New Hampshire, are now available to out-of-state residents.

10. **Encourage your child to work and save.** When your child receives cash for a birthday or holiday, urge him or her to save a portion of it. Do the same with money earned from odd jobs, chores, and summer work. Provide extra incentive to save by matching your child's earnings in a special savings account.

🔅 **Hint** The National Center for Financial Education (www.ncfe.org) has more than 40 books, games, videos, and workbooks for children of all ages. Be sure to download the brochure "18 Ways for Children or Grandchildren to Learn the Value of Money."

Scams, Swindles, and Suckers

A surprising number of perfectly intelligent people are taken in by scam artists. These seasoned cons seem to know exactly how to swindle money out of investors and savers alike. The best of them tie their pitch to current events, thereby improving their credibility and creating a sense of urgency. They often hit on the elderly, who tend to be more passive or trusting when it comes to dealing with strangers.

If You Are Elderly or Have Elderly Friends, You Should Know That . . .

- Con artists study obituaries, notices of probate proceedings, and real estate transactions to find older victims.
- Con artists know that the senior citizens often have substantial savings or proceeds from retirement plans, real estate sales, annuities, and insurance policies.
- Widowed men and women often lack experience in managing finances if their spouse took care of these matters.

- Older people are often home alone with no one to ask them to think twice about an impulsive investment.
- Older people tend to be less suspicious of strangers and more willing to invite them into their homes.
- Today's older people grew up thinking a handshake was the right way to make a business deal.

The Ponzi Scheme

A few years ago, Americans lost at least $8.3 million in a Ponzi scheme operated by a man named Hugh Rollins. He built a classic scheme around the idea of financing government contractors with promissory notes underwritten by individuals. He told investors their annual returns would be as high as 84 percent. Rollins, however, never once made the loans to the contractors and the so-called interest payments to investors actually came from money he took from new investors.

A Ponzi scheme is a swindle in which the first few investors are paid interest out of the proceeds of later investors. The latter end up with zero when the balloon bursts and the swindler pockets the remaining money. Ponzi schemes masquerade as tax shelters, deals in precious metals, diamonds, real estate, and collectibles as well as the promise to put together unique, tailor-made portfolios.

The telltale sign of a Ponzi scheme is simple—guaranteed, extremely high profits. However, there is no such thing: profits cannot be guaranteed.

Protective Steps

If you're tempted by a good-looking, fast-talking moneymaker you meet at a dinner party, a fund-raiser, or your club, before you write out a check:

1. **Make an appointment.** Visit the promoter's office. Take your lawyer or accountant with you.
2. **Get details in writing.** Show the material to both your accountant and your lawyer.

3. **Ask questions.** Insist on getting the names of at least three investors who are not relatives. Contact each and ask what, if any, return they received on their initial investment.

4. **Check with authorities.** Call your state attorney general's office, your state securities agency, and the Better Business Bureau where the promoter is headquartered to find out if complaints have been filed.

5. **Keep quiet.** Never give your Social Security, brokerage account, bank account, credit card or other key numbers to a stranger you meet or to one who calls or e-mails you.

The old cliché that if it sounds too good to be true, it probably is definitely applies.

Online Stock Scams

Remember the dialogue in *Boiler Room*, the 2000 film starring Ben Affleck as the Gen-X trader? It went something like this: "Dump those shares *now*. Let the suckers suffer. We're going to the bank!"

Although that took place on the big screen, it also happens down here in the real world . . . so often, in fact, that the SEC has a special division to deal with Internet fraud. Its regular "sweeps" continually turn up phony promoters who make millions of dollars in exchange for touting their stock on the Internet.

Pump and Dump

The most popular online scam is known as pump and dump. It occurs when clever con artists artificially inflate the price of a stock—they pump it up—and then sell it—or dump it—at its high. In their messages, which appear all over the Web—in chat rooms, on bulletin boards, in e-mails—they claim to have insider information on special company developments. Here's how the scheme works:

1. The con picks out a little known, thinly traded stock.
2. He or she buys it, starting in the morning.
3. By mid-afternoon, the con's series of purchases have driven the price way up.

4. All during this buying period, the con hypes the stock on various message boards.

5. The con then names the stock as his personal favorite on his own website or in his e-mail newsletter.

6. The price leaps up as day traders and others read the message boards and start buying.

7. The con, having entered a sell-limit order much earlier in the day, sells his shares and takes in a huge profit.

8. At the end of the day, the stock drops back to where it was in the morning.

9. The con laughs all the way to the bank. Everyone else cries.

To Avoid Getting Pumped and Dumped

BE SUSPICIOUS. If a stock is touted in a chat room or on a message board as a sure thing, ask yourself, "Why?" If it's so hot, why is someone telling everyone about it? Promises of quick profits based on tips should be ignored.

GET SEC FILINGS. The law requires that companies with more than 500 investors and $10 million in assets file reports. All companies that list their securities on a major exchange or Nasdaq also must file documents with the SEC.

Check to see if the company being touted has filed the required reports at **Edgar** (www.edgar.com). **The 10K Wizard** (www.10kwizard.com) also has quarterly and annual earnings reports.

If you can't find a company on Edgar or the 10K Wizard, call the SEC at: 202-942-8090 and ask if the company has filed under Regulation A, a regulation designed for smaller-sized firms. If it has not, don't invest.

PICK UP THE PHONE. If you're still interested but uncertain, call a company's suppliers and customers to verify that the firm is indeed running a legitimate business.

 Help! The National Fraud Exchange collects information about financial and real estate frauds from 100 government and private watchdog groups. You can run a name through the system for $39; each additional name is $20. If the person has had a complaint filed and is in the system, you'll be told on the telephone. You can also get written or faxed reports. An individual is in the system if he or she has SEC violations or infractions, fines, sanctions, or other official complaints. **Contact:** 800-822-0416.

Invest Wisely covers how to pick the right investments and avoid fraud. It's free from the Securities and Exchange Commission. **Contact:** www.sec.gov/consumer/online.htm.

The Consumer's Resource Handbook tells you what steps to take if you've been taken. It includes sample complaint letters, government agencies and their telephone numbers, hot lines, and e-mail addresses. It's free. **Contact:** 888-878-3256 or www.pueblo.gsa.gov.

The Top 25 Financial Websites

Banking

1. **Citibank Online** (www.citibankonline.com)

Comprehensive site that goes way beyond basic banking. You can read today's financial news, apply for loans, set up bill paying, e-mail money to kids via the "C2it" plan. Small Business Section covers all the basics.

BEST FEATURE: "Life's Events." Sound advice on the financial steps you should be taking if you're in college, getting married, having a baby, buying a home, retiring.

2. **Federal Deposit Insurance Corporation** (www.fdic.gov). Find out: If your bank is federally insured, what products banks sell that are *not* insured, and how to file a complaint. Excellent consumer tips.

BEST FEATURE: EDIE, the Electronic Deposit Insurance Estimator, explains which accounts are insured and which are not, and up to what dollar amount.

College: Loans, Financial Aid

3. **Sallie Mae** (www.salliemae.com). Don't be put off by the unexciting design—excellent coverage of loans, scholarships, repayment options. Calculators forecast costs and predict how much you'll need to save.

BEST FEATURE: "Financial Aid 101" gives the clearest explanations on the Web of need-basis aid and how to apply.

4. **The College Board** (www.collegeboard.org). How much college costs and how to maximize your eligibility for financial aid. Lists key dates for SAT exams and college applications. Click on "apply" for the best step-by-step guide on how to start the process and what to do when.

BEST FEATURE: "College Search." Type in the name of a school and get an in-depth profile, including application dates, type of student body, etc.

Credit Cards and Debt

5. **Bankrate** (www.bankrate.com) *The* source for finding the best savings and loan rates around the country. Articles cover a wide range of personal finance topics, from tax strategies to new types of mortgages.

BEST FEATURE: "Best Rates," a regularly updated list of interest rates at 4,000 nationwide institutions. States the best loan rates for autos, mortgages, home equity and personal loans, and the highest savings rates.

6. **National Foundation for Credit Counseling** (www.nfcc.org). This nonprofit group posts key information on such topics as how often should you check your credit card report, what to do if collection agencies are calling, and the cold, hard facts about bankruptcy. Has a useful budget worksheet and calculators.

BEST FEATURE: Links to government sites devoted to budgeting, saving, financial planning, and explanations of laws relating to credit card practices.

Government Money-Related Sites

7. **Securities and Exchange Commission** (www.sec.gov) "Investor Education" has articles and brochures about investing, protecting your money, managing a margin account, buying CDs. Also tips on how to handle problems with a broker or financial adviser.

BEST FEATURE: "The SEC Mutual Fund Cost Calculator." Allows you to quickly estimate and compare the costs of owning different mutual funds.

8. **Bureau of Public Debt** (www.publicdebt.treas.gov) Great source for information on all types of Treasuries and the differences between them—T-bills, notes, and bonds—as well as EE savings bonds. Interest rates for each are posted daily. Use the site to purchase Treasuries directly from the government. And click on "Popular Pages" for a quick overview of consumer-related topics.

BEST FEATURE: "The Savings Bond Calculators" tell what your bonds are worth, how much interest they've accumulated, and when they stop earning interest.

Investments and the Market

9. **CBS Marketwatch** (www.cbsmarketwatch.com) Although noted for its all-encompassing coverage of the stock market, the site also has savvy commentary from well-known columnists about stocks and bonds in the news. Continually updated information on U.S. and foreign markets.

BEST FEATURE: "Stock Search." Enter a company's symbol and you'll not only get the price, earnings estimate, and other current details, but also links to late-breaking company news as well as the company's profile, annual report, and brokerage firm research.

10. **The Online Investor** (www.TheOnlineInvestor.com) A justifiably popular site whether or not you own a stock. Unquestionably the best source for updates on buybacks, earnings, IPOs, stock splits, and mergers. The Tutorials will teach you how to pick winning stocks.

BEST FEATURE: "eReverent." This weekly column selects one interesting and often overlooked stock; has an excellent track record.

Kids and Money

11. **Allowance Net** (www.allowancenet.com) Lets parents and children set up an agreed-upon chore and payment schedule. Structured as a small business, the process helps kids take responsibility for assignments and watch earnings grow.

BEST FEATURE: Rate checker tool tells what other kids are getting paid for doing specific tasks. Enter the chore, how often it's done, your age, and whether you're a boy or girl.

12. **KidStock** (www.kidstock.com). Teaches kids and parents about our economy, saving money, and investing in stocks. Clear information on the types of accounts kids can open and the tax consequences.

BEST FEATURE: "Direct Purchase Plans." Lists stocks that can be bought directly from the company, with a separate listing of those with no fees.

Insurance

13. **Insurance.com** (www.insurance.com) In addition to immediate, free guaranteed quotes for auto, life, home owners, renters, liability, and disability insurance, you can also find out how to insure your boat, Harley, and pet poodle. The "Life Events" section details changes to make when you get married, divorced, have a baby, take a new job, move.

BEST FEATURE: "Ask the Experts." Pose a question and get a personalized answer.

Mortgages

14. **Microsoft HomeAdvisor** (www.homeadvisor.msn.com). An all-in-one source for anyone buying or selling a house as well as those who want to stay put. Covers financing, moving and relocation, improving your existing home, finding out what your house is worth. Continually updated chart of current mortgage rates. Locate homes for sale by zip code and price range.

BEST FEATURE: Four easy-to-use calculators: "Getting Pre-approved for a Loan," "How Much Can You Borrow?" "Buy or Rent?" and "Is it Time to Refinance?"

15. **Fannie Mae** (www.hud.gov). Best information on the Internet for first-time buyers. Explains HUD's programs that help teachers, law enforcement officers, and others buying single-family homes. Tips on working with a broker, buying a manufactured home, getting an appraisal and closing costs.

BEST FEATURE: Explanation of all types of mortgages, including the little-known energy efficient and rehabilitation mortgages.

Mutual Funds

16. **Fund Alarm** (www.fundalarm.com). Tells when to sell a fund, or at least when to consider selling. The funds on the "3-Alarm List" have underperformed for one, three, and five years. The "Honor Roll" section lists funds that have performed well.

BEST FEATURE: "What's Happening at Your Fund?" reports when a fund manager quits or is fired.

17. **Morningstar** (www.morningstar.com) The best known for its mutual fund ratings—it scans 10,000 funds for return rates and risk factors. Also offers stock quotes and general market news.

BEST FEATURE: "Portfolio X-ray." Key in your stocks and mutual funds and it will tell you how much you're paying in fees, how much is going to taxes, and if you're adequately diversified.

Personal Finance and Investing 101

18. **Moolera** (moolera.com) Geared to the twenty- to thirtysomething crowd, a great place for anyone who is starting out or wants to learn the basics about investing, real estate, taxes, student loans, 401(k)s, and IRAs.

BEST FEATURE: "Definitions." The glossary, which covers investments, real estate, and personal finance, has clear yet very thorough descriptions of basic and sophisticated concepts.

19. **Quicken**. (www.quicken.com). Very much a one-stop-covers-

all site, with good coverage of investments, bills and banking, taxes, retirement, small businesses, spending and saving, and insurance. The "Your Portfolio" section will track your stocks and send e-mail alerts when there's late-breaking news.

BEST FEATURE: Calculators: "What will you pay in capital gains tax?" "Which stock to sell to minimize taxes?" "What are your tax savings if you contribute to a 401(k)?" "What is your marginal tax rate?"

Retirement Planning

20. **Financial Engines** (www.financialengines.com). The free information, which is extensive, includes the most comprehensive yet easy-to-follow comparison of the 401(k), IRA, Roth IRA, 403(b), 457, Keogh, and SEP-IRA. Input your portfolio and receive a forecast regarding how likely it is you'll reach your retirement goals.

BEST FEATURE: "Changing Jobs" walks you through the process, including how doing so will have an impact on your retirement plan.

21. **401Kafe** (www.401kafe.com). Long recognized as *the* place for information on 401(k) plans, the expanded site now covers IRAs, market events, and news about Social Security, taxes, and money-related legislation. Ted Benna, creator of the first 401(k) plan, answers personal questions.

BEST FEATURE: The "401(k)alculator" spins out how your retirement savings will grow every year, based on your planned contributions and your expected rate of return.

Stocks and Bonds

22. **Investing in Bonds** (www.investinginbonds.com). Excellent guide for the beginning investor as well as information for serious traders. Covers: municipals, corporates, treasuries, zeros, mortgage-backed bonds.

BEST FEATURE: How to read bond prices in the newspaper.

23. **Motley Fool** (www.fool.com). A justifiably popular site

whether or not you own a stock. Ignore some of the site's silliness and focus on the continually updated news and advice about the markets and individual stocks. Has wide coverage of mutual funds, taxes, retirement issues, and personal finance topics. The "Fool's School" is a top-rate primer for beginning investors.

BEST FEATURE: "How Not to Invest." Unusually honest information about penny stocks, day trading, investment frauds, and other places where you should not put your money.

Taxes

24. **Internal Revenue Service** (www.irs.gov). In addition to being able to read and/or download all tax forms and publications here, you can also request IRS publications. Start by clicking on "Tax Info for You." Among the topics covered: who needs to file a 1040, paying your tax bill in installments, calculating your W4, and filing electronically.

BEST FEATURE: "FAQ." Answers common questions in surprisingly understandable English—such as, do I qualify for the child-care tax credit?

25. **TaxPlanet** (www.taxplanet.com). A huge but continually updated site, edited by expert Gary Klott. Has uncomplicated but thorough information on all aspects of taxes plus hard-to-find details on new and impending legislation. Discusses common and not-so-common topics such as: charitable deductions, hiring your children, the flexible spending account, capital gains taxes, and at-home office deductions.

BEST FEATURE: "Year Round Tax Guide." An easy-to-use compilation of tax tips and articles, arranged by common topics.

If You're Fired

No one, not even top executives, are immune to getting a pink slip. And no matter what your position or your salary, it's devastating. Those who planned to glide into retirement are cast adrift. Those on the fast track are suddenly derailed.

If you're one of the many Americans who has been "let go," or if you think you may be, you face a number of key financial decisions. Ideally, you have an emergency nest egg—three to six months' worth of living expenses—stashed away. But even if you don't, there are many ways to stay afloat.

Ten Steps for Handling the News

1. **Keep cool and develop a routine.** Don't panic. Problems come with solutions. And despite layoffs, there are always employers seeking employees. It may take a while to find the type of work you like, you may have to compromise somewhat, or this may be the time to shift gears and change your career.

As we go to press, there are nationwide shortages in nursing, teaching, day care (for children and seniors), health care, veterinary medicine, and dentistry. Continuing care and retirement communities as well as rehab centers and nursing homes are desperate for workers. Retail stores, restaurants, and fast-food emporiums are continually looking for intelligent workers. If you can repair equipment of any sort, from TVs, toasters, and tractors to computers, cars, and china, you can find immediate work.

To stay on track, establish a routine. Don't hang out in your bathrobe. Set up a daily morning walk or jog (with a friend so you'll keep the commitment). Or sign up for classes at a gym or your local Y. Many people keep focused and find support in morning meditation, tai chi, or prayer groups. Former employees from companies often form their own support groups; find out if this is the case with your old firm.

2. **Network.** Go to conventions, trade shows, and meetings run by associations you belong to. Talk to friends, family, and colleagues. Don't hide the fact you are unemployed. Someone you know may know someone looking for a person with your skills and talent. In addition to reading the want ads in your local newspaper and professional journals, consider turning to a headhunter or a placement firm that specializes in your area of expertise. **Korn/Ferry International** (www.kornferry.com) for example, helps executives, senior- and middle-level management people as well as college administrators and professors. **Wise Men Group** (www.wisemen.net) also specializes in executive searches as well as temporary staffing positions.

Start your search as soon as possible so you don't use up your severance pay or emergency funds.

Six places to look for jobs on the Internet:

- **Career Builder** (www.careerbuilder.com). The "Layoff Survival Kit," which includes advice for those who are forty and older who have been fired, is especially helpful.
- **CareerShop** (www.careershop.com). Will e-mail you when it finds a job match, based on the information you provide. The "Salary Wizard" calculates how much you can expect to be paid based on job and geographical location.

- **FreeTimeJobs** (www.freejob.com). Help for those who want to freelance, take on a part-time job, or work several hours a day.
- **HeadHunter** (www.headhunter.net). The most clearly organized of the sites. Search by community and location, by company, by industry. Will also e-mail you when it has a job that matches your input.
- **HotJobs** (www.hotjobs.com). Sophisticated technology lets job seekers control which employers see their resumes. Unique tools: a listing of temporary jobs, college positions, and a relocation survival primer.
- **Monster.com** (www.monster.com). Has 370,000 job postings. It recently acquired JobTrak, which has databases for more than 1,000 university career centers.

3. **Play the guilt card but be nice.** If you've been a loyal worker, the company may feel guilty about letting you go. Use this to negotiate departing perks, such as extension of your health care, a severance package, or use of an office and phone to help you search for a new job. (Companies are not required to pay severance unless this is part of the employee's written contract.)

The "be nice" part involves writing a letter to the head of your old company. (Keep a copy for your files.) Mention how much you enjoyed working there for X number of years, that you were pleased to be part of the department or team, and that you hope to reconnect in the future. This letter will not only be helpful when you give your former boss as a reference for a new job, it will also boost the likelihood of your being rehired if and when the company rebounds.

4. **Sign up for unemployment.** You and your employer have been funding this government benefit over the years and you're entitled to make use of it. It will provide a much needed short-term financial cushion.

Apply to the nearest state unemployment office immediately—you won't receive a check until all paperwork is complete and your eligibility verified. Take these three documents with you: your Social Security card, recent paycheck stubs, and a statement from your company spelling out why you were let go.

The amount you receive varies from state to state, but the general formula is 50 percent of your weekly wage, not to exceed a statutory cap. You'll get a check for 26 weeks, although when the unemployment rate is high, this is often extended for an additional 13 weeks. Most states stop coverage if you're receiving disability insurance, severance pay, or other income.

INFO: The Consumer Law Center's website at: http://cobrands. consumer.findlaw.com.

5. **Make a realistic budget and stick to it.** You must prepare for leaner times. That means skipping nonessentials, cutting back on luxury items, eating out less, carpooling, taking the bus or walking instead of jumping into taxis. And forget those cappuccinos-to-go at $3.75 each.

6. **Be straight with your kids.** Tell your children that you're out of work. If you try to hide the fact, they may imagine something much worse. Kids always sense tension at home. So explain what happened, what steps you're taking to find a new job, and what they can expect—such as they may be going to day camp rather than sleepaway. They may be going to public rather than private school. And if they're old enough, ask them for suggestions. Involving them in a constructive, non-frightening way teaches them how to handle change and take control of difficult situations.

7. **Keep severance pay in a liquid account.** Best Bet: a money market fund or short-term bank CD.

ING DIRECT, an FDIC-insured bank based in Delaware, as we go to press is paying a 3% annual percentage yield on its savings account. There is no opening minimum and there are no fees involved. Log on to: www.ingdirect.com or call: 800-ING-DIRECT.

For a high-yielding one-year CD, check rates at: **www.bankrate. com.**

NOTE: If you are given the choice of taking severance in a lump sum or in periodic payments, it's usually better to opt for a lump sum so you can invest the money and start earning interest right away. If you sense that your old firm is in financial jeopardy, the decision is a no-brainer: take the money.

✍ **Tip**: If you worked for a publicly traded company, check to see if **Moody's** (www.moodys.com) downgraded its bonds. If so, you can assume it's experiencing problems.

8. **Keep track of job hunting expenses.** Many are deductible from your taxable income under the category "Miscellaneous Itemized Deductions."

But this being the IRS, not everyone looking for work qualifies for the deductions. You must be looking for a job in the same field in which you were working.

Among the expenses to track: recruitment and agency fees, placing an ad in newspapers and journals, transportation to/from interviews, local and long distance telephone calls, and resume preparation—typing, printing, mailing. Be sure you keep detailed records, documenting your expenditures.

A word about transportation: if you are going to an out-of-town interview, your airfare, hotel, meals, taxi, and miscellaneous expenses are deductible. But don't try to turn your trip into a vacation. The IRS will be on your case.

For more details, log on to **www.taxplanet.com.** Once on the home page, click on "Select a Link" and then "Job Hunting."

9. **Keep your health insurance.** Under the Consolidated Omnibus Reconciliation Act (COBRA), companies with 20 people or more must offer employees who are losing group health coverage the opportunity to extend their coverage at group rates. Continuation lasts a minimum of 18 months, sometimes longer.

Although you pay the premiums, they will be less than if you take out your own individual health insurance policy. An exception: if your spouse has coverage, it's almost always cheaper to purchase family coverage under his or her plan.

INFO: Cobra Health Plan Advice for Individuals and Small Businesses at: www.cobrahealth.com.

If you decide to do freelance work, become a consultant, or operate your own business—and you are single or your spouse does not have health coverage—look into membership in the **National Association for the Self-Employed.** This 20-year-old organization offers group rate health insurance along with many other benefits, including online tax advice from CPAs. Call: 800-232-NASE or log on to: www.nase.org.

10. **Cash in on your medical expense plan.** If you've been contributing pretax money from your paycheck to a flexible spending account in order to cover unreimbursed medical bills, make an appointment to talk with your benefits officer. Any money left in this plan at the end of the year goes to the employer, not to you. This is informally known as the "use it or lose it" rule. Find out how your company handles the situation when employees are let go.

Among the ways you may spend any leftover money: contact lenses, an eye exam, prescription glasses, a physical, dental cleaning, prescription drugs, hearing aids, and vaccinations.

Cash in a Flash: 10 Sources Of Instant Money

In Need of Money? Where and How to Make Up the Shortfall

Maybe you bet on the wrong horse at the Preakness, had a drop-dead wedding with flowers flown in from Hawaii, or just heard from the IRS that you underestimated your taxes. Perhaps you've been laid off.

Sooner or later it happens—even to the most financially careful, fiscally conservative, and fastidious bookkeepers: the need for instant money.

A Secured Loan Is Cheaper Than an Unsecured Loan

Secured loans are those backed by stocks, bonds, Treasuries, bank CDs, savings accounts, retirement accounts, real estate or other property.

Unsecured loans are those made against your signature by a bank, credit union, credit card issuer, or loan broker. Rates are higher than on the secured version.

BankRate Monitor (www.bankrate.com) continually updates rates on all types of loans and lists the best deals around the country. And use its "Loan Calculator" to determine how long it will take to pay off your loan as well as the impact of extra payments.

1. Home Equity Loans

Borrowing against the value of your house is for many Americans the loan of choice. There are two types of home equity loans—a HELOC (Home Equity Line of Credit) and a lump sum or term loan. Both are technically second mortgages.

A HELOC is in essence a line of credit, usually with a variable interest rate. You tap into that line of credit, which has a preestablished dollar amount for the life of the loan, whenever you need money. When the line of credit has expired, everything must be paid off. Your lender may or may not allow you to renew the loan.

Lines of credit are accessed by specially issued checks or a credit card. Lenders often require that you take an initial advance when you set up the loan and withdraw a minimum amount each time you tap into it. Some even require you to keep a minimum amount outstanding.

A lump sum or term loan is a onetime lump sum that is paid off over a set amount of time, usually in monthly installments. It usually has a fixed rate of interest. Once you get the money, you cannot borrow additional money from the loan.

The Advantages: Rates are currently low and the interest is tax deductible.

The Disadvantages: With a home equity loan you wind up reducing the equity value of your home. You may be tempted to take out more than you need because getting this type of loan is relatively easy. Your house could be repossessed if you can't make the loan payments.

2. Bank CDs

You can use your certificate of deposit to secure a loan from your bank or credit union.

Or consider cashing in your CD. If it has not matured, you'll forfeit anywhere from three to six months' worth of interest, but on the other hand, you won't be running up additional debt if the CD amount covers your shortfall.

3. 401(k) Plan

More than half of all firms let employees dip into their 401(k) plan. But you must check with your plan administrator for specific details. Even those that do allow loans have differing rules and regulations.

Here's the most typical scenario:

- Your can borrow up to 50 percent of your vested balance but no more than $50,000. (Vested is the dollar amount that is yours to roll over if you leave your job.)
- Your loan must be repaid within 5 years unless you use the money to buy a principal residence. Then repayment can be made over a longer time, say 10 to 20 years.
- The interest rate is often prime plus one percent.
- There are no fees or points as they are with home equity and other loans.
- You have access to the money quickly. Very little paperwork is involved.

The Advantages: Your payments are made back into your own retirement account and not to a bank. And these payments are automatically deducted from your paycheck, so theoretically you won't miss the money very much.

The Disadvantages: The loan obviously reduces the amount you have in your plan. It also reduces the benefits of tax-free compounding. This is especially true if your employer matches your contributions.

Payments made on the are not tax deductible.

You will also be taxed twice on the loan amount. The money you borrow is money that you contributed before taxes. But you pay it back with after-tax money. Then when you withdraw the money at retirement, it will be taxed again.

If you're fired or you quit, your loan may be due immediately. If you cannot repay it, the IRS will treat the loan amount as a formal distribution and you'll have to pay federal, state, and local income tax on this money. If you're under age 59½, you'll be hit with an additional 10 percent penalty. So, for example, if you withdraw $5,000 before age 59½, you would owe a $500 penalty plus applicable federal, state, and local taxes on the entire $5,000.

However, it's possible you may not have to pay the 10 percent penalty if:

- You became totally disabled.
- You are in debt for medical exenses that exceed 7.5 percent of your adjusted gross income.
- You are required by court order to give the money to your divorced spouse, a child, or a dependent.
- You are laid off or terminated or you quit your job or take early retirement in the year that you turn 55, or later.

However, money withdrawn for any of these reasons is still subject to federal, state, and local income taxes.

☞ **Tips**:

- Borrow enough to cover what your needs are. Many companies allow only one 401(k) loan per year.
- Don't use a 401(k) loan to buy a car. Most car dealers have better rates.
- Don't use it to buy a house unless it's absolutely necessary to make up the down payment.

4. IRA

Unlike 401(k) plans, you can withdraw money at any time from your IRA. But you'll be hit with taxes. You'll pay federal taxes on your withdrawals, and if you're under age 59½, you'll pay a 10 percent early withdrawal penalty.

However, once a year you can borrow money from your IRA penalty-free—as long as you put the money back within 60 days. But miss the deadline by just a day and the full amount of the loan will be considered taxable income.

There are other situations in which you can withdraw money without paying the 10 percent early withdrawal penalty:

- To buy or rebuild a first home.
- To pay for qualified higher education costs for you, your spouse, children or grandchildren.
- If you become disabled (as defined by the IRS).
- You leave or lose your job and you're at least age 55.
- Your unreimbursed medical payments are more than 7.5 percent of your adjusted gross income.
- To pay for medical insurance when you're unemployed.

INFO: For details on tapping your 401(k) or IRA, log on to: www.401kafe.com.

5. Cash Value Life Insurance

If you have a whole life or other type of cash value insurance policy, most companies allow you to borrow 75 to 90 percent of the cash value that's built up. (Cash value is the investment or savings portion.) Rates tend to be very reasonable and you're not required to give a reason for why you want the money. You can expect a check often within 7 to 10 business days.

There's no requirement that you pay back the loan, but you should. The purpose of the policy is to protect your family should you die. If you die with the loan still outstanding, the policy's death benefit will be reduced by what you owe.

6. Stocks, Bonds, and Treasuries

You can get a loan from your stockbroker by setting up a margin account and using your securities as collateral. You could also, of course, simply sell your securities and use the cash. But if you want to hold on to your investments and sell at a better time, this type of loan is a viable alternative. The loan also lets you sidestep the capital gains taxes that might be due if you sell your securities.

Because this is a secured loan, rates are attractive. The amount is a varying percentage above the broker call rate, which currently is

5.5 percent. Your broker will give you the exact amount, but here's a typical example:

For example, if you borrow up to $24,999, the interest rate may be the broker call plus 1.99 percent. Borrow between $25,000 and $99,000 and it's broker call plus 1.50 percent. Between $100,000 and $149,000, figure on broker call plus 1.125 percent. Between $150,000 and $249,000, broker call plus 0.75 percent.

Most brokers will loan up to 95 percent of the value of U.S. Treasuries and up to 50 percent of the value of stocks. And interest paid on margin loans can be deducted against investment income.

Disadvantages: Margin loans come with a special risk. If your securities drop far enough in value, you will get what's known as a margin call. That means you'll have to cough up more collateral to keep the loan. If you don't have the cash, your only source may be to sell your stocks to pay off the loan—right at the time when your securities are falling in value.

INFO: Before borrowing against your securities, log on to the **Securities and Exchange Commission** site at: www.sec.gov. Click on "Investor Information," then on "Online Publications," and read "Margin Trading." The SEC site also has a "Margin Calculator" that spells out how likely it is that, based on your actual holdings, you'll get that dreaded margin call within the next 30 days, 3 months, or one year.

7. Your Company

Don't be shy about this one. Many companies, large and small, help employees in a cruch. The rates are around prime and you don't have to go through a credit check.

8. Banks and Credit Unions

When Willie Sutton was asked by a reporter why he robbed banks, he said: "That's where the money is." So don't forget about yours. Even if you don't have collateral, your bank or credit union may grant you an unsecured loan, depending upon your income and credit rating. Rates are anywhere from 1 percent to 4 percent higher than on secured loans, so make this a choice of last resort.

9. Credit Cards

Getting a cash advance against your credit card is, unfortunately, one of the fastest and easiest ways to get money. You put your card into an ATM or write a check and bingo, you've got what you want.

But ease is costly. Not only are rates high, but many card issuers also charge a cash advance or transaction fee which can range anywhere from 1 percent to 2.5 percent of the amount you borrow.

☞ **Tip:** Credit union credit card advances have much lower rates.

10. Family and Friends

Think carefully about turning to people you know. Make certain they are indeed in a position to part with the money. Then work out a repayment schedule and the interest amount. I recommend you pay prime, which currently is 6.75 percent. Draw up a written document, date it, spell out the terms, and then you and your generous friend or relative should both sign it.

Treat this type of loan with the same seriousness that you would treat a bank loan.

National Loan Rates

- Personal unsecured loan: 14.84%
- New car loan, 36 months: 7.94%
- Prime: 6.75%
- Broker call rate: 6.75%
- Home equity term loan: 6.70%
- Home equity line of credit: 4.75%

Your Next Steps

Now that you've read these pages you should feel comfortable in the world of finance. You should be read to add to your basic knowledge. In the style of David Letterman, here are some top ten lists to get you started.

Top Ten Books on Investing

Mary Buffett, *Buffettology: The Previously Unexplained Techniques That Have Made Warren Buffett the World's Most Famous Investor* (New York: Fireside, 1999).

John M. Dalton, *How the Stock Market Works*, 3d ed. (New York: New York Institute of Finance, 2001).

Louis Engel and Brendon Boyd, *How to Buy Stocks* (Boston: Little, Brown & Co., 1994).

Lawrence J. Gitman and Michael D. Joehnk, *Fundamentals of Investing* (New York: Addison-Wesley, 1999).

Benjamin Graham and David L. Dodd, *Security Analysis*, 5th ed. (New York: McGraw-Hill, 1988; updated by Sydney Cotile).

Michael B. Lehman, *The Dow Jones-Irwin Guide to Using* The Wall Street Journal (New York: McGraw-Hill, 1999).

Peter Lynch, *Beating the Street* (New York: Fireside, 1994).

Peter Lynch, *Learn to Earn: A Beginner's Guide to the Basics of Investing and Business* (New York: Wiley, 1977).

Martin Pring, *Introduction to Technical Analysis* (New York: McGraw-Hill, 1999).

Andrew Tobias, *The Only Investment Guide You'll Ever Need* (New York: Harvest Books, 1999).

Top Ten Magazines and Newspapers

Barron's
Business Week
Forbes
Investor's Business Daily
Kiplinger's Personal Finance Magazine
Money
Smart Money
USA Today
Wall Street Journal
Worth

Top Ten TV and Radio Stations

Bloomberg Radio
Business News Network Radio
CBS Radio
CNNfn TV
Fox News TV
NPR (National Public Radio)
PBS (Public Broadcasting System—TV)
Talk America Radio
Wall Street Journal Radio
WBIX Business Radio News

Top Ten Financial Newsletters and Research Services

Donoghue's Money Letter
Growth Stock Outlook
Hulbert's Financial Digest
Morningstar Mutual Funds
NAIC Investors Advisory Service
No-Load Fund Investor
Standard & Poor's The Outlook
The OnlineInvestor.com
Value Line Investment Survey
Wall Street Digest

Wall Street Jargon Made Simple

50 Words You Need to Know

Adjusted Gross Income (AGI): This tax-related figure is arrived at by adding up all your income for the year to get your gross income and then subtracting "adjustments." Adjustments include: contributions to qualified IRAs and other retirement accounts, alimony payments, qualified moving expenses, student loan interest, medical savings account deduction and, if you're self-employed, half the self-employment tax. Once all your adjustments have been subtracted, you have your AGI.

Asset: Something of value owned by a company (or yourself). Tangible assets are machinery, real estate, inventory, etc.; the most common intangible asset is goodwill.

Automatic dividend reinvestment: A plan in which shareholders can elect to have their dividends automatically used to purchase additional shares of stock instead of receiving a cash dividend payment.

Basis point: One hundredth of 1 percent. Used in discussing bond yields. For example, 1 percent equals 100 basis points and a yield rise from 5.04 percent to 5.50 percent is a 10 basis-point increase.

Bear market: A sharp, prolonged decline in the price of stocks. A bear fights by slapping downward with his paws, thus the phrase for a downward market.

Beneficiary: The person(s) named to receive your benefits when you die.

Big Board: Nickname for the New York Stock Exchange.

Black Monday: October 19, 1987, the day when the Dow Jones Industrial Average dropped over 500 points.

Blue chip: The common stock of a well-known national company with a history of earnings growth and dividend increases, such as IBM, General Electric, Abbott Laboratories. (In poker, the blue chips are the most valued; hence the term.)

Bond: A security that represents debt of the issuer, which can be a corporation, a municipality, or the U.S. government. Usually the issuer is required to pay the bondholder a specified rate of interest on a quarterly for a specified time. Then when the bond matures or comes due, the issuer must pay the bondholder and the entire debt known as the bond's face value. Most bonds have a face value of $1,000.

Bull market: A sharp, prolonged rise in the price of stocks. A bull attacks by thrusting upward, thus the term for an upward moving market.

Call date: A feature of many bonds giving the issuer the right to call in or redeem the bonds before their maturity date.

Cash equivalent: The generic term for assorted short-term instruments such as U.S. bills and notes, bank CDs, and money market fund shares, which can be quickly converted into cash.

Certificates of deposit: Also called CDs. Official receipts issued by a bank stating that a given amount of money has been deposited for a certain length of time at a specified rate of interest.

Compound interest: The amount earned on the original principal plus the accumulated interest. With interest on interest plus interest on principal, an investment grows more rapidly.

Custodian: The financial institution responsible for the safekeeping of your investment assets, such as your IRA.

Distribution: The income and capital gains paid by a mutual fund to its shareholders.

Dividends: A portion of the company's net profits distributed to its shareholders. Dividends are usually paid out in cash on a quarterly basis.

DJIA: Dow Jones Industrial Average. The average of the prices of the 30 leading industrial stocks. The DJIA represents the overall price movement of all stocks on the New York Stock Exchange.

Dollar cost averaging: Buying a set dollar amount of a stock or mutual fund on a regular basis. Over time, the average cost will be lower than the average price of the shares because more shares will be purchased when the price is low and fewer when the price is high.

Earnings per share: A company's net income divided by the number of outstanding shares.

Face value: Value of a bond or note when issued. Most bonds have a face value of $1,000.

Fiduciary: An individual or organization that exercises discretionary control or authority over management of someone else's money.

Index: A statistical yardstick that measures a whole market by using a representative selection of stocks or bonds. Changes are compared to a base year.

Interest: Money paid for the use of money.

IPO: Initial Public Offering. A company's offering of stock for sale to the public; a.k.a. new issue.

IRA rollover: A technique allowing employees to avoid taxes by transferring lump-sum payments from a 401(k) or other retirement plans into an IRA.

Liquid: Cash or investments easily converted into cash, such as money market funds or bank deposits.

Margin: The amount a client deposits with a broker in order to borrow from the broker to buy stocks.

Market order: An order to buy or sell a certain number of shares of a stock at the best possible price at the time the order is given.

Mature: To come due; to reach the time when the face value of a bond, note, or bank CD must be paid.

Net worth: Total value of cash, property, and investments after deducting outstanding expenses and amounts owed.

Point: A measure of a price change. With a stock, a point change means it moved up or down by $1. With a bond that has a face value of $1,000, it means a $10 movement.

Prime rate: Interest rate banks charge their largest and most financially solid business clients; it's a lower rate than that charged to consumers taking out loans.

Principal: Face amount of a debt or mortgage on which interest is either owed or earned; balance due as separate from interest.

SEC: Securities and Exchange Commission. A federal agency with the power to enforce federal laws pertaining to the sale of securities and mutual fund shares; also governs the exchanges, stock-brokers, and financial advisers.

Secondary: The market in which existing securities are traded after their initial public offering; a.k.a. the aftermarket.

Spread: The difference between a security's bid and asked prices.

Stock: A security that represents ownership in a corporation as opposed to a bond, which represents debt.

Stock split: Division of outstanding shares of stock into a larger number of shares. Splits can be 2 for 1, 3 for 1, etc.

Stock symbol: A letter or series of letters assigned to a security; used to identify issues on stock tickers. For example, the symbol for Wrigley is WWY, Tootsie Roll Industries, TR.

Street: Jargon for Wall Street and the financial services industry.

Street name: Refers to securities held in the name of the broker rather than in that of the customer.

Total return: Dividend or interest income plus any capital gain or price appreciation. A better measure of an investment's return than just dividends, just interest, or just an increase in price.

Treasuries: Bonds, bills, or notes (debt obligations) issued by the U.S. government.

Underwriter: An investment banker who agrees to purchase shares of a new issue of securities and sell them to investors. The underwriter makes a profit on the spread—the difference between the price paid to the issuer and the public offering price.

Vested benefits: The nonforfeitable dollar amount in a pension plan that belongs to the employee even if he/she leaves the job. An employee typically becomes vested after five years. Until you're vested, you cannot take your employer's contributions and earnings with you if you leave your job, get fired, or retire. You can keep all your contributions and earnings, but your company's vesting schedule will determine how much of the company's money you can keep.

Yield: The income paid or earned by a security divided by its current price. For example, a $20 stock with an annual dividend of $1.50 has a 7.5 percent yield.

Zero coupon bond: A bond that pays no current interest but is sold at a deep discount from face value. At maturity, all compounded interest is paid and the bondholder collects the full face value of the bond (usually $1,000). EE savings bonds are zeros.

Index

Abbott Laboratories, 66, 133, 140
Adjusted Gross Incomes (AGIs),
    60–62, 71, 152–53, 176–77
agency securities, 28
aggressive funds, 88
Alger funds, 27, 29, 65
Alliance funds, 117
Alliant Energy, 67, 82
Allowance Net, 163
AMBAC Indemnity Corp., 115
Ameren Corp., 82
American Century funds, 30, 74,
    92, 117, 119, 152
American Depository Receipts
    (ADRs), 140–42
American Stock Exchange, 45, 102,
    127, 132
American Water Works, 45–46,
    48
Ameritrade, 131
AT&T, 46, 111

automated teller machines (ATMs),
    6, 9–10, 37, 179
automatic savings plans, 8, 18, 20,
    49, 149–50

back-end loads, 87
balanced funds, 88, 97
bankers' acceptances, 28
Bank of New York, 133, 141
Bank One, 45, 48
Bankrate, 161, 170, 174
banks, banking, viii, 3–13, 43–44,
    71, 90, 140, 149–50
  ATMs and, 6, 9–10, 37
  CDs and, x-xi, 12, 23, 28, 38–41,
    43, 66, 170, 173–74
  checking accounts and, 3, 8, 10,
    23–26
  coupon clubs of, 7–8
  fees of, 4–5, 9–11, 25, 37
  financial calendar and, xv, xix

banks (*continued*)
    on Internet, 4–7, 160, 165
    loans and, 4–5, 10, 13, 173–75,
        178–79
    MMDAs of, x, 9, 23, 34–37, 39,
        43, 124
    retirement plans and, 58, 63,
        65–66
    safety and, 6–7, 11–12
    savings bonds and, 17–18
    selection of, 3–4
    stocks and, 49
    Treasuries and, 75–76
    windfalls and, 144
Barron's, 89, 131, 181
Better Investing, 52, 131
blue-chip stocks, 68, 101, 125
bonds, xi, 29, 35, 37, 44, 107–23
    college costs and, 112, 116, 120,
        152–53
    credit ratings of, 108, 113–14,
        118, 171
    foreign, 140, 145
    loans and, 173, 177
    mutual funds and, 26–27, 84–86,
        88, 90, 92–93, 97, 99–101, 108,
        112, 117–20, 140, 150
    retirement plans and, 66, 68, 70,
        111–12, 115, 120
    selection of, 108–10, 114–15
    websites and, 162, 165–66
    windfalls and, 145
    see also specific types of bonds
Bristol Myers Squibb, 111, 133, 140
brokers, brokerage accounts, viii, x,
        37, 141
    bonds and, 107, 110, 113–14,
        118–19
    CDs and, 40–41
    fees of, 43, 46, 54, 68, 83, 114,
        118, 129–30

    financial calendar and, xv, xxiv
    Ginnie Maes and, 93–94
    Internet and, 130–31, 162, 164
    investment clubs and, 54
    loans and, 173, 177–79
    mutual funds and, 29, 86–87,
        89–90, 93–94, 119
    retirement plans and, 58, 63, 65,
        68
    selection of, 129–30
    stocks and, 43, 46, 49, 54, 83,
        129–30
    Treasuries and, 75, 77
Brunswick Corp., 45, 48
built-in CDs, 39
bump-up CDs, 39
Bureau of Public Debt, 19, 162
BUYandHOLD.com, 48–50, 131

Calvert funds, 32, 97–98
Career Builder, 168
CareerShop, 168
CBS Marketwatch, 162
certificates of deposit (CDs), x–xi,
        12, 14, 23, 26, 38–43, 91, 112,
        124, 152, 170
    and brokers, 40–41
    checklist for, 40
    jumbo, 28–29, 38
    and loans, 173–75
    and money market mutual
        funds, 28–29, 39
    and retirement plans, 66
    selection of, 41–42
    with unique twists, 38–39
    and websites, 162
    and windfalls, 144
Charles Schwab, 77, 102–3,
        130–31
checks, checking accounts, x, xxi,
        14, 150, 179

banks and, 3, 8, 10, 23–26
  interest-paying, 23–26
  MMDAs and, 34–35, 37
  mutual funds and, 29–30, 35, 117
children, websites on, 163
Citibank Online, 160
Citizens funds, 97–98, 103
Clorox, 46, 133
College Board, The, 161
college costs, 40, 95, 151–54
  bonds and, 112, 116, 120, 152–53
  financial calendar and, xvi, xxi
  retirement plans and, 67, 152–53, 177
  savings bonds and, 17, 19
  Treasuries and, 152
  websites on, 161, 164
Columbia funds, 91
common stock, 54, 124–26
Community Bankers funds, 30
Consumer Law Center, The, 170
Consumer's Resource Handbook, The, 159
corporate bonds, 107–14, 165
  mutual funds and, 88
  newspaper listing of, 110–11
  portfolios of, 111–12
  should you buy them, 111
  zero coupons and, 121
coupon clubs, 7–8
coupons, coupon rates, 76, 109–11
  zero, 116, 120–22, 152, 165
  see also interest, interest rates
credit cards, credit card debt, 14, 150, 161
  banks and, 9–10
  financial calendar and, xiv, xix, xxi
  loans and, 173–74, 179

credit unions, 4, 13–15, 149
  CDs and, 14, 38
  checking accounts and, 14, 24
  loans and, 13–14, 173–74, 178–79
  savings bonds and, 17–18
currency exchange, 10

Datek, 131
Defined Benefit Plans, 63
designer CDs, 40
discounts, 76
Dividend Reinvestment Plans (DRIPs), 46–49, 81
dividends, 137
  mutual funds and, 85, 88, 92, 97, 101
  retirement plans and, 57–60, 67–68
  stocks and, 44, 46–49, 54, 81, 83, 123–25, 128, 132, 150
dollar cost averaging, 48–49
Domini funds, 98, 103
Dow Jones Averages, 101, 104
Dreyfus funds, 27, 31–32, 65, 89, 102–3, 97, 119
DuPont Corporation, 46, 110–11

Edgar, 158
Education IRAs, 95, 152–53
elderly, 10, 155–56
El Paso Corp., 45, 48
E-Trade, 102–3, 131
Exxon-Mobil, 47, 66, 133, 140

Fabian Investment Resource, 95
face values, 76
Federal Deposit Insurance Corporation (FDIC), 6, 11–12, 24, 36, 38, 41–42, 144, 160, 170
Federal Housing Administration (FHA), 92–93

Federal National Mortgage
    Association (Fannie Mae), 28,
    164
Federated funds, 30, 95, 103
Fidelity, Fidelity funds, 27, 31–32,
    65, 77, 89, 95, 102–3, 112, 119,
    131, 140
financial calendar, xiii-xxv
Financial Engines, 165
financial periodicals, newspapers,
    and newsletters, 88–89,
    131–33, 181–82
financial planners, financial
    planning, viii, xi, 144
  financial calendar and, xix, xxii
  websites on, 161–62
First Internet Bank, 6
First Multifund, 30
529 plans, 153
foreign investments, xix, 99–101,
    103, 139–42, 145
401Kafe, 165
401(k) plans, xi, 57, 60, 63, 69–72,
    150, 152
  loans and, 70–71, 175–77
  websites and, 164–65
Franklin/Templeton funds, 31–32,
    91, 140
FreeTimeJobs, 169
front-end loads, 87
Fund Alarm, 164

Gannett Co., 45, 48, 127–29
General Electric, 47, 133, 140
general obligation bonds (GOs),
    116
Gillette, 133, 140
Government National Mortgage
    Association (GNMA)(Ginnie
    Mae) funds and certificates,
    28, 92–95

growth and income funds, 88
growth funds, 86–87, 91, 97
growth stocks, x–xi, 44, 68
  beginner's portfolio of, 133
  investment clubs and, 54
guaranteed investment contracts
    (GICs), 70
Guardian funds, 91

Harbor funds, 92
Harley-Davidson, 66, 133
HeadHunter, 169
health care, health insurance,
    171–72
  REITs in, 138
  retirement plans and, 67, 70–71,
    176–77
  windfalls and, 144
Heinz, 46–47
Home Depot, 45, 47, 66
Home Equity Lines of Credit
    (HELOCs), 174, 179
HotJobs, 169
Hulbert Financial Digest, 132–33,
    182

IBM, 111, 140
income funds, 86–88, 97
index funds, 88, 98–104, 145
  advantages of, 100
  directory of, 102–3
  socially conscious, 98
Individual Retirement Accounts
    (IRAs), 14, 57–68, 70, 150
  advantages of, 60
  bonds and, 111, 115
  catch-up contributions to, 62
  disadvantages of, 60–61
  early withdrawal penalties of,
    59–61, 67
  Education, 95, 152–53

financial calendar and, xvii
loans and, 176–77
Roth, 61–62, 95, 165
SIMPLE, 64
top annual contributions to, 59
websites and, 164–65
industrial development bonds,
116
inflation-indexed bonds (I-bonds),
17, 74
ING Direct, 6, 170
insider trading, 133
institutional investors, 45
insurance, insurance companies,
xviii, 114, 126, 155
cash value life, 177
retirement plans and, 58, 63, 66,
70
websites on, 163, 165
see also health care, health
insurance
interest, interest rates, vii, 152, 156,
170
banks and, 4–6, 8–11, 13
bonds and, 17, 107, 109–11,
113–18, 120–22
CDs and, 38–42
checking accounts and, 23–26
compounding of, 4, 8, 10–11,
39–40, 42, 60, 175
credit cards and, xiv
credit unions and, 13–14
investment clubs and, 51–52
loans and, 4, 174–79
MMDAs and, 34–37
mutual funds and, 26, 29, 35–
36, 39, 85, 89–90, 92–93, 117
retirement plans and, 57–58, 60,
70–71, 175
and The Rule of 72, ix–x
savings accounts and, 26, 29, 37

Treasuries and, 39, 73, 76–77
websites on, 161–62
intermediate notes, 76
Internal Revenue Service (IRS),
166
international index funds,
100–101, 103
investing, investments:
basics of, 164–66
books on, 180–81
glossary of words used in,
183–87
goals for, 124, 134
as learning process, ix
of small amounts, viii-x
Investing in Bonds, 165
investment clubs, xx
how they work, 52–54
money made by, 54
stocks and, 49, 51–54, 129
Investment Company Institute,
95

job loss, 167–72
J.P. Morgan, 66, 141

Kellogg, 46–47, 67
Keogh Plans, 57, 63–65, 67, 150,
165
bonds and, 111
financial calendar and, xvii, xxiii,
xxv
types of, 63
KidStock, 163
Korn/Ferry International, 168

laddering, 112, 152
Lexington funds, 32
Liberty funds, 30
Lighthousebank, 6
Lindner funds, 91

loans:
  banks and, 4–5, 10, 13, 173–75, 178–79
  from credit unions, 13–14, 173–74, 178–79
  home equity, 174, 179
  retirement plans and, 70–71, 173, 175–77
  secured, 173, 179
  sources of, 173–79
  unsecured, 173, 179
  websites on, 161, 163–64
long-term bonds, 76

McCormick & Co., 47, 67
maturities, maturity dates, 76–77, 109–11, 113, 118, 120–21
Maytag, 45, 48
Merrill Lynch, 40, 113
Microsoft HomeAdvisor, 163
mid-cap index funds, 103
Millionaires Club, The, 53
Monetta funds, 95, 152
Money, 32, 89, 131, 181
Money Letter, The, 32
money market deposit accounts (MMDAs), x, 9, 23, 124
  comparisons between CDs and, 39
  interest and, 34–37
  rules and regulations for, 34–35
  stocks and, 43
money market mutual funds, x-xi, 23, 26–33, 84–85, 88, 90–91, 101, 124, 149, 170
  CDs and, 28–29, 39
  comparisons between MMDAs and, 35–36
  contents of, 28–29
  retirement plans and, 68, 70
  selection of, 29–30
  socially conscious, 97–98

tax-exempt, 31–33
  windfalls and, 144
Money Purchase Plans, 63
Monster.com, 169
Moody's, 108, 114
Morningstar, 89, 104, 164, 182
mortgage-backed securities, 28, 88, 92–95, 165
mortgages, *see* loans
Motley Fool, 165–66
multinational companies, 139–40
municipal bonds (munis), 107–9, 112–22, 150, 165
  liquidity of, 114
  mutual funds and, 88, 90, 117–19
  safety and, 114, 116
  selection of, 114–15
  types of, 116
  yields of, 114–15
  zero coupons and, 121
mutual funds, viii, x-xi, 45, 49, 84–104
  advantages of, 27
  bonds and, 26–27, 84–86, 88, 90, 92–93, 97, 99–101, 108, 112, 117–20, 140, 150
  buying and selling of, 89–90
  college costs and, 151–53
  fees of, 85–87, 94, 100
  financial calendar and, xv
  how they work, 26–27, 85
  for insomniacs, 90
  load, 85–87, 94
  making money with, 85
  no-load, 65–66, 85–87, 90, 94–95, 119, 140, 152
  ratings of, 88–89
  retirement plans and, 58, 61, 63, 65–68, 70
  selection of, 85–89
  socially conscious, 96–98

stocks and, 26–27, 81, 84–86,
  88–91, 96–97, 99–102, 126, 140
Treasuries and, 28–29, 74, 84–
  85, 88, 90, 92, 97
types of, 27, 86–88
websites and, 162, 164, 166
windfalls and, 145
*see also specific types of mutual
  funds*

National Association for the Self-
  Employed, 171–72
National Association of Invest-
  ment Clubs (NAIC), xx, 47
National Association of Investors
  Corp. (NAIC), 52–53, 131
National Association of Securities
  Dealers' Automated Quotation
  (NASDAQ) market, 45, 101–2,
  104, 127
National Center for Financial
  Education, 154
National Foundation for Credit
  Counseling, 161
National Fraud Exchange, 158–59
Negotiable Order of Withdrawal
  (NOW) accounts, 23–26
net asset values (NAVs), 85, 94
NetBank, 7
networking, 168
Neuberger & Berman funds, 65, 92
NewsCorp, Ltd., 45, 48, 141
New York Composite Index, 102
New York Stock Exchange (NYSE),
  45, 101–2, 110, 127, 132
No-Load Investor, The, 95, 100,
  182
Nuveen funds, 118–19

Online Investor, The, 162
open-ended mutual funds, 85

Parnassus funds, 97
par values, 76
Pax World funds, 97
penalty-free CDs, 39
Pep Boys, 82, 133
PepsiCo, 47, 133, 140
Pioneer funds, 97
Ponzi schemes, 156
price to earnings (P/E) ratios, 126–28,
  132
primary market, 45
prime rate, 71, 179
procrastinating, xi
Procter & Gamble, 46–47, 133, 140
Profit Sharing Plans, 63
prospectuses, 86, 89
pump and dump scam, 157–58

Quicken, 164–65

Real Estate Investment Trusts
  (REITs), 67, 99, 103, 137–38
recall risk, 109–10, 113
redemption fees, 87
repurchase agreements (repos), 28
retirement plans, retirement accounts, xi, 45, 57–72, 95, 100,
  152–53
  bonds and, 66, 68, 70, 111–12,
    115, 120
  custodians for, 65–68
  early withdrawal penalties of,
    59–61, 67, 176–77
  loans and, 70–71, 173, 175–77
  as necessity, 57–58
  stocks and, 66–68, 70, 126
  websites and, 164–65
  *see also specific types of
    retirement plans*
revenue bonds, 116
rollover rates, 42

Roth IRAs, 61–62, 95, 165
Rule of 72, The, ix-x
Russell Indexes, 100–102, 104

salary-reduction plans, 69
Sallie Mae, 161
saving, savings, savings accounts,
    vii-viii, x-xi, 26
  automatic deposit plans for, 8,
    18, 20, 49, 149–50
  in banks, x, 3–5, 7–8, 10–11, 23
  in credit unions, 13
  for emergencies, x
  goals for, viii, xi, xiv
  interest and, 26, 29, 37
  investment clubs and, 52
  MMDAs for, 36
  painless techniques for, 149–50
  of small amounts, x
  see also retirement plans, re-
    tirement accounts
Savings Incentive Match Plan for
    Employees (SIMPLE), 64
scams, 144, 155–59
Scudder funds, 119, 140
secondary market, 41, 45, 118
  Treasuries and, 75–77
sector funds, 88
Securities and Exchange Commis-
    sion (SEC), 86, 109, 141,
    157–59, 162, 178
Security First Network Bank, 7
senior citizens' programs, 10
Series EE Savings Bonds, xi, 16– 20,
    23, 49, 91, 121, 150, 152, 162
severance pay, 170
Shering Plough, 45, 48
Sherwin-Williams, 45, 48
Simplified Employee Pension Plans
    (SEPs), 57, 63–65, 111, 165
  financial calendars and, xviii, xxiii

single-state bond funds, 118–19
small-cap index funds, 100–101, 103
Southern Co., 47, 67
Standard & Poor's (S&P), 125–26
  bonds rated by, 108, 114
  indexes of, 54, 88, 99, 101–2, 104
  The Outlook of, 182
  Stock Guide of, 125, 132
  Stock Reports of, 83, 132
Stein Roe funds, 91, 152
stock purchase plans, 47–48, 150
stocks, stock market, 29, 35, 37,
    43–54, 76, 81–86, 114, 143,
    150, 153
  beginning portfolio for, 123–34
  buying of, 44–50, 129
  definition of, 43–44, 81, 124–25
  dollar cost averaging with,
    48–49
  emotional traps in investing in,
    133–34
  finding information on, 131–33
  foreign, 99, 140–41, 145
  game plan for investing in, 134
  hometown, 82–83
  investment clubs and, 49, 51–54,
    129
  loans and, 173, 177–78
  making money in, 44
  mini-investor programs for,
    43–50
  mutual funds and, 26–27, 81,
    84–86, 88–91, 96–97, 99–102,
    126, 140
  readiness for investing in, 124
  reading financial page listings
    of, 127–29
  retirement plans and, 66–68, 70,
    126
  safety and, 81, 124, 130
  scams and, 157–58

selection of, 124–27, 130
of utility companies, xi, 44,
    81–82
websites and, 162–63, 165–66
Stratton funds, 92
Strong funds, 27, 66, 89, 91–92, 95,
    102

taxes, 50, 52, 171
    bonds and, 17, 19, 107, 111–22,
        150
    CDs and, 39
    college costs and, 151–53
    financial calendar and, xiii–xxv
    loans and, 174–77
    mutual funds and, 31–33, 87–88,
        90, 100, 153
    retirement plans and, 57–64,
        68–72, 111, 115, 150, 175–76
    scams and, 156
    Treasuries and, 39, 73–76, 111
    websites on, 161, 163–66
    windfalls and, 144
Tax Planet, 72, 166, 171
T.D. Waterhouse, 90, 131
teaser rates, 42
10K Wizard, 158
Texaco, 46–47
Treasury bills, notes, and bonds, xi,
    23, 26, 73–77, 94, 123, 150
    auctions for, 75, 77
    basics on, 75–76
    buying of, 77
    and comparisons between CDs,
        39
    definition of, 74–75
    inflation-indexed, 17, 74
    and loans, 173, 177–78
    and MMDAs, 35, 37
    and mutual funds, 28–29, 74,
        84–85, 88, 90, 92, 97

and retirement plans, 68
and safety, 73, 75, 107, 111
and websites, 162, 165
and windfalls, 144
and zero coupons, 121, 152
Treasury Direct System, 77
T. Rowe Price funds, 31–32, 66, 89,
    95, 112, 119, 140, 151
TV and radio stations, 181
12b-1 fees, 86–87

unit investment trusts:
    bonds and, 108, 114, 117–20
    single-state, 118–19
    tax-exempt, 117–20
USA Today, 42, 89, 131, 181
U.S. goverment income funds,
    88
utility companies:
    bonds of, 111–12
    stocks of, xi, 44, 81–82

Value Line, 83, 102, 125, 132–33,
    138, 182
Vanguard funds, 31–32, 89, 92, 95,
    100–104, 112, 118–19, 140
Van Kampen funds, 119
Veribanc, Inc, 11–12
Veterans Administration (VA),
    92–93

Walgreen, 67, 133
Wall Street Journal, 32, 42, 74, 89,
    131, 181
Washington Public Power System,
    114
websites, 160–66
wills, xi, xxiii, 144
Wilshire Equity 5000 Index, 101–
    2, 104
windfall investing, vii, 143–45

Wise Men Group, 168
Wrigley, 45, 48, 67, 133, 140

yankee CDs, 28
yields, 5, 150
    bonds and, 107, 109–11, 114–15,
        117, 119, 121–22
    mutual funds and, 89, 94, 97, 117

REITs and, 138
stocks and, 125–26, 128

zero coupon bonds, 120–22, 152,
    165
    how they work, 120–21
    munis and, 116
    types of, 121

About the Author

Nancy Dunnan has been writing about the world of finance for over twenty years. She appears regularly on CNN, Business News Network, Bloomberg Radio, and National Public Radio in New York City. In addition to *How to Invest $50-$5,000*, she is the author of *Dunnan's Guide to Your Investments, Never Call Your Broker on Monday, Never Balance Your Checkbook on Tuesday,* and *Never Short a Stock on Wednesday*. She also writes monthly columns for *Bottom Line Tomorrow*, BuyandHold.com, TheOnlineInvestor.com, and www.HomeAdvisor.msn.com.

Nancy was awarded the Distinguished Service Award in Investment Education from the Investment Education Institute, an affiliate of the National Association of Investors Corp. A native of Ft. Dodge, Iowa, and with degrees from Simmons College and Case Western Reserve University, she now lives in Manhattan—on a budget, of course.